D1622854

Fun & Easy Crosswords

Our award-winning and very fun crossword puzzles from celebrity authors just for you in a practical book to solve anywhere at any time! All these puzzles have been highly rated with at least 4 stars out of 5 by the American crosswords community (including thousands of avid players).

Important info: For the player's convenience are the clues continued on the left hand side in case they do not fit on the first page. E.g. the main grid of puzzle #10 is printed on page 22, whereas the remaining clues are continued on page 21. This way the player does not have to turn the page while solving the puzzle.

Publication © 2018 by Henning Dierolf.
All rights reserved.

Contact e-mail: henning@devarai.com
Website: www.devarai.com

ISBN-13: 978-1724275165
ISBN-10: 172427516X

Contents

Devarai CROSSWORDS

It's About Time

by Elizabeth C. Gorski

Copyright © Devarai GmbH

ACROSS

1 "___ with the Wind"
5 Casual conversation
9 Baseball hats
13 Civil rights org.
15 Singer ___ Del Rey
16 Help with a heist
17 When a procrastinator might do something
20 Mathematical proposition
21 Religious sch.
22 Golf legend Snead
23 Enlist again
25 Cain's brother
27 Synagogue leader
31 James Bond portrayer ___ Brosnan
34 Snoozing
36 Last number before "Liftoff!"
37 Opposite of naughty
41 Volume II of Churchill's book series "The Second World War"
44 Secured with needle and thread
45 The Browns, on scoreboards
46 More tightly stretched
47 O-ring, for example
50 Very impolite
51 Tuscan city with a leaning tower
53 Lopsided win
55 Prohibit
56 Apt. divisions
59 More expensive
64 Fourth of July
67 Astronaut Armstrong
68 Drench
69 Conquer a crossword
70 ___ dunk (basketball power shot)
71 "Dancing Queen" band
72 Beholds

DOWN

1 Biting insect
2 Hand-on-the Bible vow
3 NBA's Archibald
4 Reverberating sound in a cave
5 Stop talking
6 Celine Dion's "A New Day ___ Come"
7 Wee picnic crashers
8 Docile
9 Tuna or ham container
10 Harsh treatment
11 Flower segment
12 Slender wine glass part
14 Bubbly water brand from France
18 "To Kill a Mockingbird" author Harper ___
19 All-in-one Apple computer
24 Trailblazer
26 Epic Charlton Heston film of 1959
27 Charlie Brown's "Darn it!"
28 Tennis great Arthur
29 Erupted, as a volcano
30 Human ___ (earthlings)
32 Opposite of WSW
33 Sit down and relax
35 USMC ranks
38 Very small amount
39 Pool hall sticks
40 Makes a mistake
42 Variety or type
43 Military maneuvers
48 Seniors' advocacy org.
49 Capital of Kansas
51 Talk-show group
52 Pakistan's neighbor
54 Coffee vessel at a breakfast meeting
55 Trash collectors?
57 Southwestern land formation
58 Nose-in-the air type
60 Corporate VIPs
61 "Spamalot" creator Eric
62 Roof overhang
63 Deli breads with seeds
65 Stately tree
66 Small dollop

Monster Mash!

by Elizabeth C. Gorski

Copyright © Devarai GmbH

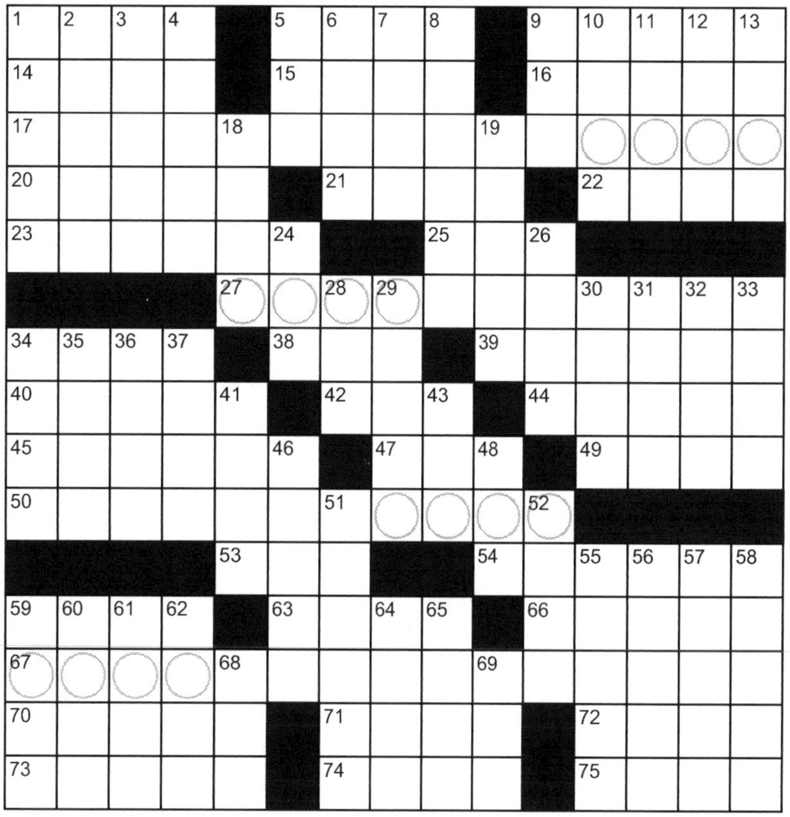

ACROSS

1 Boutique
5 Wearing nothing
9 ___ the Hutt ("Star Wars" villain)
14 ___-Cola (Pepsi rival)
15 Figure skater's jump
16 Cupid's missile
17 Washington D.C. power couple during the Clinton years
20 Noisy fight
21 Drench
22 Has debts
23 Old Testament book with 150 parts
25 Bro's kin
27 Western route for some pioneers
34 Paradise
38 Lyricist Gershwin
39 Popular search engine
40 Seriously annoys
42 $ dispenser
44 Picnic spots
45 Celebrity chef who yells "Bam!"
47 "Alley ___"
49 Catholic church service
50 Director of "The Witches" and "Two Deaths"
53 Raw rock
54 Mixed, as a salad
59 Buffoon
63 Diploma earner, briefly
66 Very beginning
67 Back-friendly furniture for office workers
70 Beetle Bailey's boss
71 "Garfield" pooch
72 Elm or oak, for example
73 Rain-snow mixture
74 Cathedral area
75 Bygone fliers

DOWN

1 Rascal
2 Swiss cheese features
3 City northwest of Orlando
4 Talk-show group
5 Black Halloween critter
6 Graph line
7 Seized vehicle
8 Texas border city
9 Pickle holder
10 Jason's ship
11 Arched facial feature
12 Yawn-inducing speaker
13 Dazzles
18 Audition CD
19 Making do, with "out"
24 ___ Lanka
26 "Go no further!"
28 Notable time
29 Croc's kin
30 Wander about
31 Taj Mahal locale
32 Types
33 Minus
34 On the level?
35 "Ghost" actress Moore
36 Corp. bigwig
37 Infamous emperor
41 Missile shelter
43 Cattle call
46 Florida's Key ___
48 Teacher's fave
51 Sunday talk
52 Painter Vincent van ___
55 Plane assignments
56 Uses a swizzle stick
57 White-plumed wading bird
58 Rx amounts
59 Own (up)
60 Verbal
61 Monster who's anagrammed in four places (see the answers with circles)
62 Opera house section
64 Tragic Verdi heroine
65 604, in old Rome
68 Tennis court divider
69 So-so grade

Autumn Relay

by Elizabeth C. Gorski

Copyright © Devarai GmbH

ACROSS

1 To boot
5 Marry
8 He's totally evil
13 "Star Wars" princess
14 "Rah!"
15 Like ewes and hens
16 Make retroactive, as a check
18 Mortgage source
19 Short sock
20 Rejuvenating resort
22 Old U.S. gas brand
23 Initial poker payment
25 "Famous" cookie man
27 Daredevil's feat
30 2010 comedy film starring Steve Carell and Tina Fey
35 Frog's habitat
36 Groan-producing wordplay
37 Less distant
38 Reduced quantity?
39 Meals in the park
41 Raw rock
42 "Pop Goes the ___"
44 Support org. for GIs
45 "Terrible" time for tots
46 Day's end
48 Investment choices
49 Oboe insert
50 "Be that ___ may ..."
52 "Star Wars" knights
55 Stephen of "The Crying Game"
57 Baseball great ___ Reese
61 Pumpkin color
63 Alternative plan for Autumn?
65 Connected
66 Actress Longoria
67 Post marathon soreness
68 Poke fun at
69 Drenched
70 Sticky substances

DOWN

1 "Dark Angel" star Jessica
2 Trimmed of fat
3 Tired partner?
4 San Francisco Bay city
5 Lawman Earp
6 Grab a bite
7 Hair colorings
8 Observe
9 Jason Bourne's memory malady
10 Tiny amounts
11 Pub drinks
12 Roman emperor
15 Passionate Spanish dance
17 Fender bender
21 Bit of butter
24 PTA concern
26 Tip jar fillers, mostly
27 Reproduce, like salmon
28 Oscar-winner Marisa ___
29 Remove ID from, as a Facebook photo
31 Void a marriage
32 Not a kid anymore
33 King of Judea
34 Lock of hair
36 Stole, as from a supply closet
39 Tennis star Sampras
40 Cuba, to Cubans
43 Gets smaller
45 Pledge drive carryall
47 Citric beverage
48 Jessica of "7th Heaven"
51 Dreaded sound at an egg toss
52 Sudden shock
53 Great Lake with the shortest name
54 Comedian Carvey
56 Not many
58 Texas city
59 Sound effect in a canyon
60 Squeezes (out)
62 Kin of "Golly!"
64 Rd. crosser

Shades of Blue

by Elizabeth C. Gorski

Copyright © Devarai GmbH

ACROSS

1 Texter's "Wow!"
4 Capital of Azerbaijan
8 Top story?
13 Cow's greetings
15 Divisible by two
16 Lose ground?
17 Legumes used in hearty soups
19 Played at a casino
20 Opening remarks
21 Snoozer's noise
23 Sheep's plaint
24 ___ Jima
26 Exile isle
27 Latvia or Estonia, on old maps (Abbr.)
28 "Promising" event planned for Prince Harry and Meghan Markle
33 "Mean Girls" actress Gasteyer
34 Deadly sin
35 ___ many words
39 Dunk into water
41 Popeye's salad choice
44 Not as expensive
45 H.S. math course
46 Golf legend ___ Snead
47 Twangy stringed instruments
52 Upscale German auto
55 Pac-12 sch.
56 ___-fi (literary genre)
57 Fan's cry
58 Weavers' machines
60 "Madam Secretary" star Téa
64 Suspect's excuse
66 Explosive situation
68 Shoulder bag part
69 New York canal
70 Fill up a piggy bank
71 Epsom ___ (foot-bath additive)
72 Brit. Airways jets, once
73 "Are we there ___?"

DOWN

1 Prefix with "potent" or "present"
2 Zombie's groan
3 The "G" of G Man (Abbr.)
4 Spelling contest
5 Gardner and DuVernay
6 Eisenhower's successor
7 Still available for purchase
8 Sea off Greece
9 ___-la-la
10 Mausoleums
11 Concepts
12 Fragrant wood used for hope chests
14 Aleppo's land
18 Alley athlete
22 Baseball stat
25 Possesses
28 Train track
29 ABBA's "Take a Chance ___"
30 Orange veggies
31 Lady of Eden
32 Tonic's mixer
36 Apollo 13 org.
37 Al Capone's facial feature
38 Electric resistance units
40 Curvy letter
41 Droop
42 Opposite of minus
43 It may hang around the house during winter
45 Makes a lot of noise
48 Colorful Dutch flowers
49 Earth-friendly prefix
50 Runs off to marry
51 Cake layers
52 Orchestra section that includes tubas
53 Island nation near Sicily
54 Spin
59 Loretta of "M*A*S*H"
61 "Agreed!"
62 Actress Campbell
63 "___ a Kick Out of You"
65 Flying Halloween critter
67 ___ Moines, Iowa

Celebrity Chef Favorites

by Elizabeth C. Gorski

Copyright © Devarai GmbH

ACROSS

1 Pricey Super Bowl broadcast spots
4 Grand tale
8 Puppeteer Lewis
13 Fibs
15 Eric of "Troy"
16 Yucatán native
17 Salad morsels endorsed by actor Kevin?
19 Track legend Jesse
20 Doorway
21 Game with a jackpot
23 Fuss
24 Props for Monet and Manet
26 Shabby
28 Pasta topper endorsed by comedian Ray?
33 Bummed out
36 Smoke detector?
37 Malia Obama's sister
38 Advanced math
40 Donates
43 Ocho ___, Jamaica
44 On the briny
46 Ruler of Qatar
48 Decompose
49 Mexican snacks endorsed by actor Sean?
53 Eloise's hotel, with "the"
54 Dark and gloomy
58 Page in a road atlas
60 Specialized vocab
63 "Still Alice" Oscar winner Julianne
64 "Old MacDonald" refrain
66 Halloween treat endorsed by comic actor John?
68 Commuter line with a bar car
69 Leer at
70 Shoelace snarl
71 Haunting
72 Sun beams
73 Soon-to-be grads

DOWN

1 "Tiny Alice" playwright Edward
2 Mother of William and Harry
3 Factions
4 Flow out
5 Water bucket
6 Division word
7 Cuba's Fidel
8 Irons (out)
9 Hem and ___
10 Sailor's reply to a captain
11 "Atlas Shrugged" author Ayn
12 ___ many words
14 More achy
18 Parachute material
22 Tic-___-toe
25 Urban haze
27 Eye drop
29 "___ was saying ..."
30 "Over my dead body!"
31 "Beat it, gnat!"
32 Sunrise direction
33 Wild guess
34 Museo display
35 Vanish
39 Mil. bigwig
41 Brit. record label
42 Uses a chair
45 Edible mollusk
47 Spacious
50 Submachine gun
51 Animosity
52 Painter's garb
55 Unexpected benefits
56 Goof
57 Payments to a landlord
58 Apportion
59 Suffix with million or billion
61 Lady ___ (pop diva)
62 Roy Orbison's "___ the Lonely"
65 Three, on a sundial
67 ___ Moines, Iowa

Devarai CROSSWORDS

Looking for Hired Help

by Elizabeth C. Gorski

Copyright © Devarai GmbH

ACROSS

1 Sombreros and berets, for example
5 Appear (to be)
9 Duos
14 Start of a magic spell
15 Killer whale
16 Borden spokescow
17 Aoraki/___ (New Zealand's highest peak)
19 Soar like an eagle
20 Take to court
21 Here, in Paris
22 Actor who played Lou Grant on TV
24 Manhattan area with an annual film festival
27 Language suffix
28 Scottish-born "A Family Man" actor
33 Fancy neckwear
36 Yoga class pads
37 ___ de toilette (perfume)
38 Entryway
39 Gooey lumps
41 Broken-bone protection
42 Boxing legend nicknamed "The Greatest"
43 Some chorus voices
44 Pub projectiles
45 "Good Will Hunting" actress
49 "My lips ___ sealed!"
50 Made into law
53 ___ manner (doctor's behavior)
57 ___-mo (replay speed)
58 Miss Piggy's pronoun
60 Crop up
61 Rita's occupation, in a Beatles song
64 Fey and Turner
65 "___ a Kick Out of You"
66 Aachen article
67 Pig's nose
68 Spinning toys
69 Pond growth

DOWN

1 Some Easter meats
2 ___-face (180° turn)
3 More loyal
4 ___ Francisco
5 World Cup sport
6 Beethoven's Third
7 Green prefix
8 Create
9 Winged horse of myth
10 Ready for action
11 "The check ___ the mail"
12 Theme park attraction
13 Crystal gazer
18 Nepal's neighbor
23 Unpaid bills
25 Composer Stravinsky
26 Large cabinet for clothing
29 Wee dollop
30 Shakespearean king
31 Sunrise direction
32 Boring routines
33 Eve's mate
34 Single-voice arias
35 Penny, nickel or dime
39 Run, as colors in the wash
40 British "Inc."
41 Golfer's vehicle
43 Most ventilated
44 Interior design
46 Bahamas capital
47 Arched part of the foot
48 Parking attendants
51 Online letters
52 "Nothing ___!" ("Forget it!")
53 Winged cave mammals
54 Ms. Brockovich
55 Flintstones' pet
56 Send forth
59 Creative thought
62 Prima donna's problem
63 ___ culpa

House of Cards

by Elizabeth C. Gorski

Copyright © Devarai GmbH

ACROSS

1 Casual runs
5 Exams
10 "___ the night before Christmas ..."
14 Kind of collar or circus
15 Honda luxury car
16 Lion's share
17 Color worn on St. Patrick's Day
19 "___ Excited" (Pointer Sisters hit)
20 Thoroughly soak
22 "You've got mail" co.
23 Bonkers
26 Dan Brown's "The ___ Code"
28 Tennis match division
29 Socialist Marx
32 Quarterback Manning
33 Balloon filler
34 Mascara worry
36 "Blue Bayou" singer Ronstadt
39 Mellows
41 Heroic tales
43 Hollywood clashers
44 Sassiness
46 Flood protection
48 Ottawa's prov.
49 Menlo Park monogram
50 500 sheets
51 Sultry singer Peggy ___
52 Methods
56 James of "The Blacklist"
58 '60s war zone
59 New England team
62 "Sad to say ..."
64 Joaquin Phoenix played him in "Walk the Line"
68 "Star Trek" captain
69 ___ knee (proposing)
70 Finished
71 Candy Crush snowman
72 Lay down the lawn ... again
73 Orange pekoe and Earl Grey

DOWN

1 NYC airport
2 Flamenco cheer
3 Solidify
4 Zesty dip
5 Wrestling duos
6 Beige
7 One who says, "See you in court!"
8 Tire pattern
9 Pole star?
10 Texter's "I've heard enough!"
11 2015 Helen Mirren/Ryan Reynolds film
12 Formal club (Abbr.)
13 Vodka brand, familiarly
18 Tugs abruptly
21 Daring Knievel
23 Sir ___ Newton
24 Horsy "hello"
25 Wise to urban living
27 "Would ___ to you?" (swindler's query)
30 Not faux
31 Pub choice
35 Terrific review
37 Recipient of a gift
38 Fall flower
40 Padded bicycle part
42 Flavored with salt and pepper
45 Retain
47 Ready for a refill
52 Serpentine
53 Connecticut Ivy Leaguer
54 Military rank
55 Diamond or ruby
57 Fancy neckwear
60 Frat letters
61 ___ time (right away)
63 Enjoy Aspen
65 Wide city street (Abbr.)
66 Vast expanse
67 60-min. units

Super Starts

by Elizabeth C. Gorski

Copyright © Devarai GmbH

ACROSS

1 Young cow
5 Coral formation in the sea
9 Salary increase
14 River to the Baltic Sea
15 Mystique
16 '50s TV star Stu
17 Hostile takeover
19 Showy spring flower
20 Obey, with "by"
21 Island country in the Indian Ocean
23 "Certainly!"
24 Poorly lit
27 Water cooler?
28 Ideal member of society
34 Angelic ring
37 Large bird of Australia
38 Wear away, as topsoil
39 Landed
40 Main artery of the heart
43 Charged bits
44 "From ___ shining ..." ("America the Beautiful" lyric)
46 Dawn goddess
47 ER doctor's "ASAP!"
48 Long lunch?
52 Cause for extra innings
53 Slangy refusal
54 ___ Zeppelin (rock group)
57 Discouraged
62 Cara or Castle
64 Dangerous bacteria
65 Barrier-breaking noise caused by an aircraft
68 Funnel shaped
69 Mystical sign
70 Long division word
71 Potato-filled deli snack
72 Broadway light
73 Observes

DOWN

1 Patient's share of a doctor's fee
2 Hacienda brick
3 "Elmer Gantry" author Sinclair ___
4 Dance legend Astaire
5 Cleaning cloth
6 Germany's continent (Abbr.)
7 Historic periods
8 Rayon or cotton, for instance
9 Jam-packed (with)
10 Location
11 Lottery player's victorious cry
12 Porcelain kitchen fixture
13 One-named "May It Be" singer
18 Decorate anew
22 Here, in Dijon
25 Notion
26 Bit of office correspondence
28 Slogan's relative
29 Enticed
30 ___ coffee (bar order)
31 Kind of suit
32 Tracy's mom in "Hairspray"
33 Home that's made of twigs
34 Corned beef dish
35 Protected, at sea
36 One who tells fibs
41 Word with meeting or hall
42 Thailand's continent
45 Swift-running bird of Africa
49 Balloon filler
50 "Taken" actor Liam
51 Stylishly elegant
54 Sierra ___ (African nation)
55 Short message via PC
56 Audition CDs
57 Pack of cards
58 Business school course (Abbr.)
59 Nobel-winning author Morrison
60 Yale students
61 Rounded roof of the Capitol
63 Baseball stats
66 Prefix for liberal or conservative
67 Rural hotel

What Halloween Creatures Use

by Patrick Merrell

Copyright © Devarai GmbH

ACROSS

1 One of the world's first fruit tasters
5 Spill the beans
9 Ice skating figure
14 Temptress in "Damn Yankees"
15 Peru's capital
16 Golfing great Sam
17 Liquid that "eats"
18 Sign of things to come
19 Bombards, as with snowballs
20 What Halloween creatures use to get into haunted houses?
23 African country where Barack Obama Sr. was born
24 Susan of "The Partridge Family"
25 Choreography move
29 TV break fillers
30 Drain, as energy
33 Puts leftovers in the microwave, e.g.
35 Spooky
37 Dwarf tree
38 What Halloween creatures use to get around in swamps?
41 "Smile, you're on '___ Camera'!"
42 Chuck Berry's "Johnny B. ___"
43 Gasoline ratings
45 Conflict that took place about 100 yrs. ago, for short
46 Suffix meaning "sorta"
49 Nobody
50 "Homeland" org.
52 Cheese-covered chip
54 What Halloween creatures use to create horror stories?
58 On the ocean
61 Root used in Hawaiian cuisine
62 Cafe au ___
63 Make a latte design, e.g.
64 Times worth remembering
65 Rotating rod on the road
66 Blue Ribbon beer maker
67 Ready for picking
68 Worried investor's order -

DOWN

1 State number 49
2 Linked, as spacecraft
3 Invaders in a sci-fi movie
4 Passionately, in love
5 Psychologist's ink pattern
6 Ride with lots of legroom inside
7 Alter a statement
8 One doling out Monopoly money
9 Cable TV athletic award
10 Basically
11 Type of toothpaste
12 Hairdo hider
13 Scores usually followed by one-pointers, briefly
21 Enters gradually
22 Facial feature darkened with a pencil
26 Undertaking
27 When flts. are due in
28 Tire inflation abbr.
31 1930s architectural style
32 Pizzeria order
34 Escape artist Harry
35 Puts at risk
36 Work unit
38 Anti-mugger spray
39 Aware of
40 Haul off to the repair shop
41 One who cuffs crooks
44 Your mom's daughter
46 Helpful tool on a glacier
47 Irritatingly high-pitched
48 Youth or elder follower, in lodging
51 Creator of Pong and Centipede
53 Book with an index of places
55 Stop
56 Cylindrical sandwich
57 "The Bachelorette" ceremony offering
58 Nile snake
59 Pan Am competitor
60 Rival in the fam, often

51 McDonald's clown

53 Become fond of

55 Penguin suits

56 Like free checking accounts

60 Revered figure

61 Escher and Hammer

62 "Aladdin" prince

63 "___ hear" ("That's what they tell me")

65 Plural form of "is"

66 Learnin' basics, briefly

Devarai CROSSWORDS

Puzzle 10
www.devarai.com

A California Christmas

by Patrick Merrell

Copyright © Devarai GmbH

ACROSS

1 Rodeo rope
6 Seized car, for short
10 Worker's week-ending cry
14 Follow, as a hunch
15 Like dedicated fans
16 When tripled, "et cetera"
17 Honkers in a gaggle
18 Tree with needles and cones
19 "Hey, buddy" sound
20 Bring-a-dish meal
22 Co. bigwig
23 "Nope"
25 California town that sounds like a good place to avoid cold weather
29 "Happy Days" character clad in a black leather jacket
31 Wade's courtroom opponent
32 Angsty music genre
33 Dangle
34 Atop, in poems
36 It's a notch above a C+
38 California neighborhood synonymous with the movies
41 Law enforcement officers
44 Nosh on
45 Canadian gas brand
49 Nickname for the star of "Selena"
50 Home of Fin. and Ger.
52 A, C or D, in a pill
54 California city with a famous pier
57 Employ
58 Item in a holster
59 Like coatings on diving boards
61 Harpo or Karl
63 Box with a combination lock
64 ___ Allan Poe
67 Detective's lead
68 Bullfight chants
69 "___ is human ..."
70 Moral failings
71 Worrisome March day
72 Having a few more rings around the trunk

DOWN

1 Pool shot to see who breaks
2 Card designated by one large pip
3 Physicist Hawking or novelist King
4 Neither great nor terrible
5 Left jab, hard right combo
6 Fairy tale character with a "golden stair" of hair
7 Throw out of an apartment
8 Like a medium steak, vs. one that's well done
9 Laudatory poem
10 Like a workaholic's personality
11 Baking appliance with a pilot light
12 Photo badges, for short
13 Butcher trimmings
21 Once-popular kitchen flooring
22 Cancer treatment, briefly
23 Ultimate degree
24 "That's it!"
26 Field dealing with automatons
27 Large Australian bird
28 Calculator figs.
30 String between E and J
35 Loaf that might have caraway seeds
37 Notion
39 Most of the earth's surface
40 It can be enhanced using large hair curlers
41 Sleepwear, briefly
42 Bran or gran suffix
43 Short term's opposite
46 Smeared, as a pastel drawing
47 Bro's counterpart
48 Hydrogen's atomic number

59 In addition
60 Jared of "Dallas Buyers Club"
61 Notable periods
63 Guy's barn dance partner
64 "Honest" prez
65 Sharp turn

A Couple of G's

by Patrick Merrell

Copyright © Devarai GmbH

ACROSS

1 Like duck feet
7 Writer Edgar kicked out of West Point in 1831
10 Rankles
14 First-birthday milestone
15 Calif.'s largest airport
16 "Nothing ___!" ("A piece of cake!")
17 San Francisco bridge named for the strait it crosses
19 "I'm ___ here!"
20 Tivoli's Villa d' ___
21 Type of garden with raked gravel
22 Tweak
23 Female immortalized on the Acropolis
27 Attack violently
30 Simple
31 Phrase on a Chinese menu
32 Rogen or Meyers
34 Painting, dance, etc.
38 School website ending
39 Crafter's plug in tool
42 Sometimes dreaded conjunction
43 Signals some doggy happiness
45 Norwegian capital
46 Throw in one's two cents
48 Ambiance
50 Polish pact city
51 Charades or Twenty Questions
56 Leader of the pack
57 Make some dishes disappear
58 Story
62 "___ Wonderful Life"
63 Car seen often at the pumps
66 City defeated by a wooden horse
67 Muscles below the pecs
68 Spanish snooze
69 ___ Club (Costco competitor)
70 Actor DiCaprio, to friends
71 Domes near Nome

DOWN

1 $10 an hour, for example
2 Swelled heads
3 Buckled band
4 Corner stores in a barrio
5 Opposite of WSW
6 Washington of "Fences" and "Training Day"
7 Last place a pirate might walk
8 Cereal grain
9 PC file suffix
10 "Shoulda listened to me"
11 Paper boy's path
12 Fliers with strings attached
13 Shapes on a general's helmet
18 "Golly!"
22 Station break fillers
24 Diana of "On Her Majesty's Secret Service"
25 Very beginning
26 Pearl Harbor site
27 From the top
28 Big Gulp liquid
29 Annoyingly self-satisfied
32 B. Anthony on a dollar coin
33 Wriggly swimmer
35 Stats for a MLB slugger
36 "Sorry Charlie" fish
37 Beefy bowlful
40 Actress Loughlin or Petty
41 Linguist whose first name is an anagram of "moan"
44 Struts in a showy way
47 Twisted snack food
49 U.S.S.R.'s Cold War foe
50 '60s dance whose name comes from Africa
51 Trot and canter
52 Violet or marine prefix, for an artist
53 ___ salts (bath product)
54 Canvas preparation
55 Practical joke

Thanksgiving Dinner Scavenger Hunt

by Patrick Merrell

Copyright © Devarai GmbH

ACROSS

1 Tour de France mountains
5 Most numerous chess pieces
10 Salt, symbolically
14 Rainy day preparer of fame
15 It can cause a cook to cry
16 Soothing tissue additive
17 Pillow filler
20 Blockbuster
21 Door in the floor
22 Belly
23 Honshu Island port
25 Caustic substance
27 Frank of the Mothers of Invention
31 Thrift store transactions
33 The ___ Affair (political episode)
35 Chip shot's path
36 Broadway orchestra area
37 Compete
38 Helpful handhold for a rope climber
39 Sofa frequenters
43 "Cat on ___ Tin Roof"
44 Gigayear
45 Lancelot's title
46 Egg carton count (abbr.)
47 Pitching-machine piece
48 In a state of tranquility
52 Dork
54 Chum
56 Its flag symbolizes a rising sun
57 Part of mph
59 Princess warrior of TV
61 Like Mother Hubbard or King Cole
62 Bolts of furniture fabric
67 Chico or Karl
68 Units transformed by a transformer
69 Prefix with meter, for a pilot
70 Predator's quarry
71 Deputized pursuers
72 Ruler length

DOWN

1 Tattoo for Popeye
2 Tina of "Gilligan's Island"
3 Ziti and penne
4 Sound from a librarian
5 Penniless
6 Historical records
7 Very thin, as hair
8 Negative word
9 Tucked in
10 Can./U.S./Mex. pact
11 Boxer who floated like a butterfly
12 Hoodwink
13 Rockette's "kicker"
18 Slanted, as type
19 Tennis ball covering
24 Busted beyond repair
26 Lit-up theater sign
28 Window segment
29 Seasoned performers
30 Play a part
32 Early anesthesia
34 Ingredient used to make bread or beer
37 Maria ___ Trapp
38 North or South follower, in the Far East
39 Grub
40 Seep
41 Circumstance's partner
42 Container on a coffeehouse counter
43 Do sums
47 Cain's brother
48 Warns
49 Moon mission program
50 Beckon from afar
51 Breaks things off
53 Strong glue
55 Skating jumps
58 Answer an invite
60 NASDAQ competitor
62 Official that might be hit by a foul tip
63 Number posted on a golf tee
64 Charlemagne's realm (abbr.)
65 As well
66 Bumbler

Devarai CROSSWORDS

Puzzle 13
www.devarai.com

May the Workforce Be with You

by Patrick Merrell

Copyright © Devarai GmbH

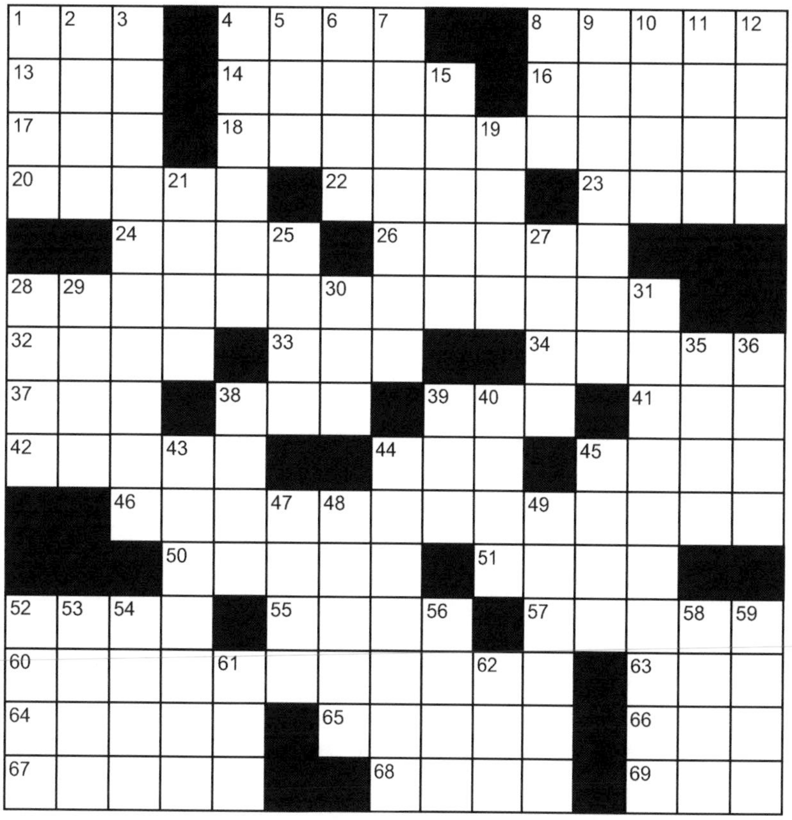

ACROSS

1 Pablum-covered neckwear
4 Pizazz
8 Bookcase part
13 Whom Uncle Sam wants
14 Creme-filled cookies
16 Backyard party locale
17 UFO pilots
18 Table server clad in all black?
20 Verbally greet
22 Bug bugging a beagle
23 Monthly payment
24 Enjoy a long bath
26 Mary-Kate or Ashley
28 Bun-headed carpet installer?
32 Enormous
33 Started, using a match
34 Piano exercise
37 Noise
38 Fitting
39 Partner of hers
41 No-goodnik
42 Traffic bottleneck
44 Heckler's holler
45 White House worker
46 Idealistic young man armed with a pooper scooper?
50 Like pets, as noted on their tags
51 Astounds
52 Cola or root beer
55 Slushy drink brand
57 Fancy necktie
60 Hairy writer on a home computer?
63 "Yuck!"
64 The world's most famous Grouch
65 Had a tantrum
66 Bikini top
67 Japan's capital
68 Mama's boys
69 Always, in poetry

DOWN

1 Automatic tournament advancements
2 Tiny bit
3 Sound made by a phone without call waiting
4 Aries-to Pisces system
5 Tax-deferred plan, for short
6 Spongy ball brand
7 Made oneself scarce
8 Masseuse-hiring business
9 Lunch lady's headwear
10 Luncheon or major suffix
11 Property claim
12 Old West outpost
15 Seashore find
19 "Fuzzy Wuzzy ___ ..."
21 Sharpen, as one's skills
25 Large seaweed
27 Pair behind a pair of glasses
28 Degs. for many profs
29 Wreck
30 Get on a ride on mower, for example
31 3-D puzzle with nine squares per side
35 Vacationer on a horse ranch
36 The "E" of FEMA (abbr.)
38 ___-Seltzer
39 Non-sharing type
40 Big corn state
43 Flee on foot
44 Barrio grocery stores
45 Pub pours
47 Disney's "___ and the Detectives"
48 Interior designer's specialty
49 Emmys and Grammys
52 Many a Highland games competitor
53 "___ that's what you've been up to!"
54 Fifty-two cards
56 Frozen waffle brand
58 Fairy tale brute
59 "___ she blows!"
61 Sis's counterpart
62 Suffix with hallow

Favorites on the Playlist

by Elizabeth C. Gorski

Copyright © Devarai GmbH

ACROSS

1 Job-safety org.
5 Sugar servings (Abbr.)
9 Rain delay covers
14 ___ Cong
15 "Star Wars" critter
16 Visitor from another planet
17 "Sad to say ..."
18 "Piece of cake!"
19 Starr of the Beatles
20 Neil Diamond hit of the 1980s
23 Thanksgiving veggies
24 Chowed down
25 Nonstick cooking spray
27 Sailor's "Yes!"
29 "Kidnapped" monogram
30 Comedian Margaret
33 Pacific, for one
35 Gather, as crops
37 Where Cleveland is
38 Irving Berlin song that's featured in the Fred Astaire film "Blue Skies"
41 Russian river
42 Rim
43 Mrs. Eisenhower
44 Chum
45 ___ kwon do
46 Wee dollop
48 Scoreboard abbr.
49 Guggenheim Museum display
50 Ms. McEntire
52 State song of Kansas
59 Momma's mate
60 Z ___ zebra
61 Shirt brand that once had a croc logo
62 Velocity
63 Father, to a baby
64 Tilt to one side
65 Watches over
66 God of war
67 "Gone Girl" actress Ward

DOWN

1 Cameo shape
2 Missile shelter
3 Black Sabbath's rock genre
4 Totally bewildered
5 Wee
6 Sultan of ___ (Babe Ruth)
7 Very fancy
8 Terrier type
9 Mystical decks of cards
10 Girl in Wonderland
11 Ice hockey locale
12 Wooden pins
13 ___-Caps (movie candies)
21 Saudi's neighbor
22 "Polo" designer Lauren
25 Annoying online ad
26 Honda's luxury car
28 Lose ground?
29 Assessed
30 Intelligent arboreal ape
31 Bandleader's shout
32 Moves like goo
34 The Braves, on scoreboards
36 Chang's brother
37 "Is it a boy ___ girl?"
39 "Swell!"
40 Glowing bit in a fireplace
45 Tire patterns
47 Sports venues
49 Intensified, as sound
51 Leaves quickly, in slang
52 "___ springs eternal"
53 Word on a store sign
54 Zilch
55 Russian ruler of yore
56 Conceal
57 Soccer announcer's cry
58 Author Ferber
59 Calif. clock setting

Letters of Affection

by Elizabeth C. Gorski

Copyright © Devarai GmbH

ACROSS

1 Yoga class pad
4 Comic Roseanne
8 Center of Florida?
13 Sugary suffix
14 Judges wear them
15 Wear down
16 Props that are opened at the Academy Awards
19 "The Crucible" setting
20 Spinning toys
21 Bulletproof garment
22 USO show attendees
24 In the past
26 How some ice cream cones are served
33 ER doctor's "ASAP!"
35 Farm unit
36 Vowel group
37 Foot rub response
38 Scandinavian liquor
40 SSW opposite
41 Doom's partner
43 Comfy-cozy
44 Swear
45 1999 Barbra Streisand album
48 Notable time
49 Capote nickname
50 Sharif of "Dr. Zhivago"
53 Come clean?
57 Spanish buddy
61 Revealing memoir by a former sweetheart
64 Gathered leaves
65 Rx amounts
66 "Born in the ___"
67 Stubborn critters
68 Affectionate acronym spelled out by the first words of 16-, 26-, 45- and 61-Across
69 Bashful

DOWN

1 Fuzzy rock cover
2 On the briny
3 Blue shade
4 Physique
5 Help a crook
6 Nevada city
7 "Please reply" abbr.
8 Slithery fish
9 Stir up trouble
10 Deal (with)
11 Poetic tributes
12 Try out
14 Word on an invoice
17 Sanctioned
18 Actor Morales of "Criminal Minds"
23 Cager O'Neal, for short
25 Bitty biter
26 "Yippee!"
27 "Pardon me," in Italy
28 April 1 gag
29 Cabaret show
30 "Peanuts" boy
31 Billions of years
32 Takes to court
33 Long story
34 Starbucks latte size
38 North or South continent (Abbr.)
39 "___ Rhythm"
42 Supervise
44 Tiny cake remnant
46 Mower's target
47 Russian mountain range
50 Gumbo veggie
51 Farrow and Hamm
52 Requests
54 Tosses in
55 Pack cargo
56 "For ___ jolly good ..."
58 Debtors' notes
59 "Holy cow!"
60 Say yes to
62 TV spots
63 Currency of Albania

49 One with a flintlock, stock and long barrel
50 Queen or dean
51 Resulted in
52 Help in a heist
53 Depend (on)
54 Outdoor furniture wood
55 Workplace fuel for Bob Cratchit
56 Light and bright
57 Stir up
58 Recipe amts.

The Missing Suit

by Patrick Merrell

Copyright © Devarai GmbH

ACROSS

1 Open-handed swat
5 Pooch parts with pads
9 Fictional detective Charlie
13 It borders Ore. and Ariz.
15 Saddam Hussein's land
16 "There's no place like ___"
17 Name said when addressing an Amazon Echo
18 Expert
19 Smartphone booked ride service
20 Place with a plate and three bases
23 Flood barrier, such as in New Orleans
24 Door knocker sound
25 Trio preceding UV
28 Like many who get soc. sec. checks
29 Victoria's Secret purchase
30 "Break me off a piece of that Kit ___ bar"
33 In the company of
35 Pool stick
36 Verdi opera set in Egypt
37 Private facility, usually requiring dues
41 Rum-laced cake
42 Disaster relief
43 Ring-shaped reef
44 Surgery sites in hosps.
45 Extended NFL periods
46 Punch sound in a comic book
48 French holy woman (abbr.)
49 Spitfire-flying grp. in W.W. II
50 Proceeding for Perry Mason
52 Blood-pumping implant such as the Jarvik-7
59 Old Wendy's slogan: "Where's the ___!"
60 Kid's punishment, perhaps
61 Goodbye in Guadalajara
62 Airline headquartered in Israel
63 Healthy salad green
64 Sunset or Vegas follower
65 Little kid
66 [Spoiler alert] What Rosebud is in "Citizen Kane"
67 Olive and Castor in "Popeye"

DOWN

1 Strike-breaking worker
2 "___ Land" (wrongly named Best Picture winner at the 2017 Oscars)
3 Quaffs for Robin Hood and his Merry Men
4 Computer-image unit
5 Small friend of P-P Pooh
6 As ___ (normally)
7 Hospital section
8 Neighborhood nut hoarder
9 One played for a fool
10 Tramp
11 Prayer ending
12 Geek
14 Maker of expensive, decorated eggs
21 Baltic or Vermont follower in Monopoly (abbr.)
22 League just below the Majors
25 Machine gun toting Stallone character
26 Lipstick mishap
27 Mummy sites
29 Whopper topper
30 Olympic weightlifting amounts, briefly
31 No longer a minor
32 Restaurant booth alternative
34 Rockets and Pistons org.
35 Cape ___, Mass.
36 Play a part or part of a play
38 No-good tattlers
39 Female sibling, for short
40 Some Japanese motorcycles
45 Bungler
46 Faced with courage
47 Feel the pain

"Recording" Artists

by Patrick Merrell

Copyright © Devarai GmbH

ACROSS

1 William Tell's target
6 In a day ___ (soonish)
10 Eve's partner
14 Salad dressing bottle
15 Shakespeare: "The lady ___ protest too much"
16 It's about 1600 meters
17 CD on a CD
19 Country between Turkey and Afghanistan
20 Sci-fi beings
21 Descriptive wd.
22 Pencil tip
24 "Right now!," in a hospital
26 Rolls out a new lawn
28 Prestigious prize
31 Country between Turkey and Jordan
33 Semi-hurried, as a walking pace
35 Suffix with infant
36 Bathing suit top
38 Freud topic
39 Variety show segment
40 DVD on a DVD
43 Boxer biter
45 Prepare to throw a dart
46 "___ we there yet?"
47 A day in Spain
48 One in the plus column
50 Bunch of bees
54 Go back for more salsa
56 Eye part
58 Gin fizz fruit
59 Be skeptical about
61 Actress Long or Peeples
63 Pea holder
64 Pathetically purse one's puss
66 LP on an LP
69 Machu Picchu resident
70 Highlands tongue
71 Group of experts
72 Mouse-sighting yells
73 Cold War country (abbr.)
74 Mower "garages"

DOWN

1 Entry
2 Attractive
3 Star emitting electromagnetic radiation
4 Flowery neckwear
5 Sicilian smoker
6 Goldfinger's bowler-hatted bodyguard
7 "Vive le ___!" (old French cry)
8 Octagon on a corner
9 "Dear me!"
10 Essential ___ acids
11 Off-road motorcycle
12 Chicken ___ king
13 Guys
18 Mag. heads
23 Printing-cartridge filler
25 Leg bone next to the fibula
27 Starry-eyed sort
29 Quarterback Manning
30 Rent
32 Cannonball's path
34 Scotch mixer
37 Aliases
39 Slants
40 Goner
41 Not the home team players
42 Nos. on wine bottles
43 Four-term U.S. prez
44 Fib
48 "The Simpsons" Kwik-E Mart clerk
49 More petite
51 Skiing category
52 Shared an apartment (with)
53 Olympic awards
55 Smidgens
57 Your mom's daughter, briefly
60 Cordon ___
62 iPhone purchases
64 Rhubarb or pecan dessert
65 Start of a count
67 Letters before Enterprise on an aircraft carrier
68 Cheer syllable

67 Meet, as a poker bet

Double Talk

by Patrick Merrell

Copyright © Devarai GmbH

ACROSS

1 AM/FM device
6 Fuss
9 Like some exclusive communities
14 Kenneth Lay's scandalous energy company
15 Burger or dog holder
16 Last letter of the Greek alphabet
17 Short non-eating periods?
19 Type of whale
20 Every breath you take
21 Co. head honchos
23 Countdown start, often
24 AOL alternative
27 Bulbs that don't weigh much?
30 "My fingers are crossed!"
32 Toxic clean up org.
33 Mex. miss
34 Mississippi, in relation to the Mississippi River
37 Mendes and Longoria
40 Local ocean movements, at the moment?
44 Software test version
45 In ___ (as found, in archaeology)
46 Idaho and New Mexico borderer
47 Savings plan initials
49 Stops daydreaming
51 Undistinguished flatlands?
56 Tree that sounds like you
57 "Har har," in textspeak
58 Music player that debuted in 2001
59 Heart test letters
61 One more time
63 So-so carnivals?
68 Phrase on a Chinese menu
69 Celeb's rep.
70 Protective atmosphere layer
71 Muscle areas in need of kneading
72 Football kicking aid
73 Find a new purpose for

DOWN

1 Whistleblower, in the N.B.A.
2 Request at an Alabama game: "Gimme ___!"
3 Ones making hosp. rounds
4 Smidgen
5 Already in the books
6 Muscles between the pecs and the quads
7 Word after Pennsylvania or double
8 Beginning
9 One spreading rumors
10 Fuse box unit
11 Set surrounding the tongue
12 "Snowy" wading bird
13 Denounces strongly
18 Up and out of bed
22 Soccer stadium cheer
24 Leftovers category (abbr.)
25 Small bush
26 ___ Dame University
28 Billies and nannies
29 Threw in the towel
31 Second segment of a miniseries
35 ___-fi
36 "Hotel Rwanda" people
38 Nervous
39 One of 48 contiguous ones
41 Income
42 Marathon competitor
43 Hour or half hour TV offering
48 Smartphone add-on
50 Request
51 It might be walked on a pirate ship
52 Enter an Internet password, say
53 Famed San Antonio mission
54 Lite
55 Saying
60 Look into a crystal ball
62 Minimal suffix
64 Meteor suffix
65 Debt note
66 Health-care pros

67 Waffle brand in the freezer
69 Skin design, slangily
70 Dearie
71 Can. province on Lake Superior

Long Odds

by Patrick Merrell

Copyright © Devarai GmbH

ACROSS

1 Woes
5 Branch
9 Headquartered
14 600-year-old ark builder
15 Suffix with switch or sock
16 Aunt's cohabitant
17 Eisenhower or MacArthur, in World War II
20 Firing ___ cylinders
21 Advertising maxim: "___ sells"
22 Light bulb unit
23 Glasses wearer, disparagingly
27 "Give ___ break!"
28 Dangerous snake
31 Doubled, an African fly
32 Con game
34 "Do you love me or do you not? / You told me once but I forgot," for example
36 String between D and H
38 Paycheck fattener
42 Ringling Bros. and Barnum & Bailey offering, for many years
46 John Philip ___, aka the March King
47 Dove's call
48 Retain
49 "Pronto!" letters
52 Monopoly properties located 5, 15, 25 and 35 spaces from GO (abbr.)
54 Porker's pen
55 ___-fi
58 Unsolicited opinion
61 "Gone with the Wind" estate
63 Type of fees in a gated community (abbr.)
64 Otherworldly
68 Superstore's gas-saving advantage
72 Craze
73 School for James Bond
74 "Groovy, man"
75 Skirt crease
76 Car door imperfection
77 Concerning

DOWN

1 The "I" in F.Y.I., for short
2 Pork cut
3 Molten rock
4 Library book's resting spot
5 "Serve again" tennis call
6 Lyricist Gershwin
7 Man famous for his dots and dashes
8 Just-over-par scores
9 Hamburger holder
10 Again from the beginning
11 "Vamoose!"
12 Gladden
13 River mouth formation
18 Piggy bank opening
19 Corp. board member
24 Computer manual reader
25 New mortgage deal, informally
26 Woman's wrap in Mumbai
28 Bldg. rentals
29 Artsy NYC neighborhood
30 "Land of the Inca"
33 X or /, in bowling
35 Small plateau
37 Health supplement chain
39 Frozen Italian treats
40 Fat in a feeder
41 Annual cable sports award
43 Boston-to Barcelona heading
44 Bill Clinton's vice president
45 Husk-y vegetable
50 Dr. Seuss's "Horton Hears ___"
51 Tuckered out
53 Staircase part
55 Walk heavily
56 Amsterdam houseboat docking site
57 Woman's name meaning "peace"
59 Hindu social class
60 Brown tone used in old photos
62 Home to the Black Sea and the Yellow River
65 Clears
66 Monogram part (abbr.)

![Devarai Crosswords]

Devarai CROSSWORDS

Creature-featured

by Patrick Merrell

Copyright © Devarai GmbH

ACROSS

1 Wedge for a margarita
5 Colorful parrot
10 Jimi Hendrix hairdo
14 Credit card co. nickname
15 Main Street establishment
16 Radar screen spot
17 With feet pointing inward
19 Madly mouth off
20 Obstacle when combing
21 Response that can lead to "I do"
22 Composure
23 El ___ (Spanish hero)
25 Bookmarked, in a way
27 Away from a delta
31 Curtail
32 Flexible, like some lamps
35 First Lady Perón
38 Mechanic's grease job
39 Paternity-test stuff
40 Rates ___ (is perfect)
41 What candles on a kid's cake represent (abbr.)
42 Brave
46 A tick of the clock, briefly
47 Place to purchase pots and plants
48 Nutty
53 Fish eggs
54 Command to Rover
55 Brook add-on, for a NYC borough
57 Keep one's bedmate awake, say
61 Pub amount
62 Stubborn
64 Obligatory poker bet
65 "Practice makes perfect," e.g.
66 The horizon, in a drawing
67 Thick and thin suffix
68 Tightly packed
69 Observed

DOWN

1 Swimmer's training routine
2 Joiner's phrase
3 Prefix meaning "big"
4 Gym activity
5 AOL alternative
6 Legal pro (abbr.)
7 Whispered sweet nothings
8 "Am not!" response
9 Marry
10 Overseas
11 Knack
12 Middle step when shampooing
13 Chose (to)
18 Gal in "Popeye" cartoons
22 Remain in limbo
24 TV room
26 "Golly!"
27 Hideous
28 Fill coffee or tea cups
29 Burgles
30 Overhaul, as decor
33 Anderson Cooper network
34 Madeline of "Young Frankenstein"
35 Suffix with cigar
36 Zig or zag
37 Amos's old radio partner
40 Military storage sites
42 Potato soup flavorer
43 Like a frosted mug
44 Where Belg. and Bulg. are
45 Got up
46 Pair for a hockey player
48 Channel covering the U.S. House
49 Give one's views
50 Pennies
51 Evade
52 Singer Bob awarded the 2016 Nobel Prize in Literature
56 Strips used in a darkroom (abbr.)
58 "Garfield" pooch
59 Surrealist Magritte
60 Garden with a talking snake
62 "Spy vs. Spy" magazine
63 Giggler's syllable

Devarai CROSSWORDS

"Bible Jeopardy: What Beasts!"

by Kelly Clark

Copyright © Devarai GmbH

ACROSS

1 Actor Joe of "My Cousin Vinnie"
6 High point
10 Invitation letters
14 Bygone Apple messaging software
15 Heroic deed
16 Suit to ___ (be ideal): 2 wds.
17 Old codgers
18 Capital of Italia
19 Some cameras, for short
20 This grasshopper's cousin plagued Egypt: 4 wds.
23 Austere
25 Huron and Erie, e.g.
26 In Daniel, one, like a lion, had this bird's wings.: 4 wds.
30 "Long time, ___!": 2 wds.
31 Sicilian volcano
32 Palm reader, e.g.
33 Safe place
35 Wife, in Germany
39 Detective's assignment
40 Christmas songs
41 Look out...they sometimes come in sheep's clothing.: 3 wds.
45 Atlantic or Pacific
47 More dangerous
48 Abram was rich in these beasts of burden.: 3 wds.
52 Cairo's river
53 Big name in car rentals
54 Used oars
57 ___'acte (intermission)
58 Tennis's Sampras
59 Destructive 2011 hurricane
60 Cheers from the stands
61 Winter riding toy
62 "Bad, bad" Brown of song

DOWN

1 Photo, briefly
2 Environmentalist's prefix
3 Display piece
4 Medical tube used to remove fluid
5 "The score is even!": 3 wds.
6 Zimbabwe's continent
7 Corporate heads: Abbr.
8 Baby's first word, maybe
9 And others, for short: 2 wds.
10 Imp
11 Inspired author of Acts: 2 wds.
12 Poem part
13 Ants in the pantry, e.g.
21 "___ the season to be jolly"
22 Gymnast Korbut
23 Barley beards
24 Sneaker or loafer
27 "When pigs fly!"
28 Summer on the Seine
29 ___ Arbor, Michigan
33 Derby or fedora
34 Cool ___ cucumber: 2 wds.
35 Traditional tales
36 Movie critic, say
37 On the safe side, at sea
38 Gorbachev was its last leader: Abbr.
39 Scene of Jesus' first miracle
40 Nasal opening
41 Riches
42 Extremely intolerant sorts
43 Used the rubber end of a pencil
44 Cleverness
45 Deed holder
46 Fine dinnerware
49 Emulates Eminem
50 Stuntman Knievel
51 Give as an example
55 Brian of ambient music
56 Actress Susan of "The Partridge Family"

62 Early filmmaker Fritz

65 Qty.

66 What a priest, a rabbi and a duck might walk into

67 Word used to frighten

One Word, Two Words

by Patrick Merrell

Copyright © Devarai GmbH

ACROSS

1 Misgiving
6 Ship's front
10 A brown fruit or bird
14 Beneath
15 "I didn't mean to do that!"
16 Apple desktop computer
17 Make an inspirational guide laugh?
19 Relocate
20 Kenan's TV partner
21 Neatnik ... not!
22 White skinned, green-haired Batman foe
23 Suffix with bachelor
25 Fastens with a click
28 Surfing?
33 Elroy's dog in "The Jetsons"
36 Boycott
37 Brit's bathroom
38 Glittery appliqué
41 Winter Olympics ramp
44 Hole in one's head?
45 Class where pipe cleaners and Popsicle sticks might be used
47 Uneven, as a road
48 Approximately 18 holes of golf?
53 Motel 6 competitor
54 Final notice in the newspaper, briefly
58 Hunky-dory
61 Item carried by Jack and Jill
63 Air Force or Marine follower, for the president
64 Away from the wind, when sailing
65 Pertaining to a prize fight?
68 Fly like an eagle
69 Grain used in making beer
70 "Negative, captain"
71 Word on half a towel set
72 Tom, Dick and Harry, for example
73 Must, slangily

DOWN

1 Earth-rumbling disturbance
2 Not reached, as goals
3 One paying full price, usually
4 "___ Miserables"
5 Battlefield rations (abbr.)
6 College in Claremont, California
7 Purple-stalked plant used in pies
8 Clip-___ (armless sunglasses)
9 Misery
10 Japanese robe
11 "Don't worry about me"
12 Visually say hello
13 Worker who writes with a pastry bag
18 in addition
22 Nine-to-five activity
24 Bring in, as a salary
26 Kisses and hugs for all to see, for short
27 Went to the bottom of the ocean
29 Swamp
30 Reunion attendee, briefly
31 Frolic
32 Sluggish from taking medications
33 In the middle of the ocean
34 Argue (with)
35 Root used to make poi
39 Tramp's partner in a Disney title
40 Historical periods
42 "Son of," in Arabic names
43 Martial art in the Olympics
46 "From the Halls of Montezuma/ To the shores of ___"
49 What milkers get milk from
50 "No" vote
51 Flying without a pilot's control
52 Yard or meter
55 Give a leg up
56 Alaskan native
57 Aquarium fish named for its square fins
58 Short race
59 Gel from a spiky succulent
60 Close by

Sounds Like It

by Patrick Merrell

Copyright © Devarai GmbH

ACROSS

1 Johnny who played Captain Jack Sparrow
5 Old witches
9 Blessing before a meal
14 List-ending abbr.
15 Common ingredient in lotions
16 ___ Ingalls Wilder
17 Play to ___ (draw)
18 Person, place or thing word
19 Looks at, in a creepy way
20 Old-fashioned friend?
23 Gal's partner
24 Sailing across the Atlantic
25 Quandary
29 Type-A males
34 Frazier's three time boxing opponent
35 Tyler Perry character
38 Assist
39 Farm female that runs haphazardly?
43 Longoria and Peron
44 "Are not!" comeback
45 Brit's bathroom
46 Protected
49 Thorton Wilder play that's an anagram of "worn out"
51 Lenin's land, for short
54 Massage
55 "Will do, Mr. Bear"?
63 Flood barrier
64 Frozen beverage brand
65 Wearing one's birthday suit
66 Gives off
67 Like a Jekyll/Hyde personality
68 Therefore, to a logician
69 Bowling result that's unlikely to yield a spare
70 Feudal lord's lackey
71 Meat and potatoes dish

DOWN

1 Unhearing
2 Woeful words from Caesar
3 Coughed up the dough
4 Fundraising promise
5 Mr. fix-it sort
6 Moises or Jesus of baseball
7 Dutch cheese
8 Transmits
9 Worldwide
10 Popular spaghetti sauce brand
11 "___ Lang Syne"
12 Street reputation, slangily
13 Uncomplicated
21 Scrumptious
22 Nay's opposite
25 Olympic gymnast Dominique
26 "As ___ and breath!"
27 Light purple flower
28 Sarah McLachlan hit
30 ___ Beta Kappa
31 Title word before Dolly
32 Permit, to happen
33 Secretly watch
36 Dutch or American tree
37 High male singing voice
40 Baton Rouge sch.
41 "Go ahead, see for ___"
42 Discussion site
47 Having the least manners
48 Paul Anka's "___ Beso"
50 Steakhouse orders
52 Screeches to a halt
53 Fix a pool stick
55 Bullfight cheers
56 Dole's presidential running mate, Jack
57 Sinister
58 Abominable Snowman
59 Number on a wine label
60 Vonnegut or Cobain
61 Rim
62 "Ouch!"

Fantasy Football Teams

by Elizabeth C. Gorski

Copyright © Devarai GmbH

ACROSS

1 Arm or leg
5 Video-game pioneer that created Asteroids
10 Came to rest on a flower
14 Composer Stravinsky
15 Italian city that's a fashion hub
16 Oscar-winning actress Sorvino
17 Chicago team that trains in the Arctic?
19 Smith or Wawrinka of tennis
20 Shorthand pro
21 Clean with a broom
23 "For shame!"
24 Initials for the self-employed
26 Furnace fuel
28 Business-oriented New York team?
34 Punk rock offshoot
36 Worry compulsively
37 "Right back ___!" ("Likewise!")
38 Pharmaceutical giant Eli ___
40 IRS employee
41 Pitchfork part
42 White House staffer
43 Common voicemail message
45 Wide shoe letters
46 Well-read Detroit team?
49 "Topaz" author Leon
50 Capote nickname
51 "It's c-c-cold!"
53 Abu ___
57 Boise's state
61 Mighty trees
63 Tress-free Philadelphia team?
65 Done with
66 On ___ (winning big)
67 List-ending abbr.
68 Piano's 88
69 Anti-establishment type
70 Nitwit

DOWN

1 Where you apply ChapStick
2 "___ Rhythm"
3 Burrowing critter
4 "The Godfather" star Marlon
5 Embassy VIP
6 Father's Day gifts
7 "There oughta be ___!"
8 Scarce
9 They can really bug you?
10 Early hrs.
11 Small digits?
12 Savings plans, briefly
13 Propane container
18 Scottish folk hero, or the name of a cocktail
22 "The Bells" author
25 LAPD alert
27 Slightly open
28 One way to kick a habit
29 Tinseltown trophy
30 Answer an invitation
31 Angry ___ get out (fuming)
32 Daly of "Judging Amy"
33 Wise one
34 Airline to Tel Aviv
35 1003, in Old Rome
39 Lusty look
41 Famously mainstream Illinois city
43 Where there are no free spirits?
44 "Good Will Hunting" sch.
47 Free (of)
48 Elbowed gently
51 Library purchase
52 5-star film review
54 Swiss river
55 Amorphous sci-fi villain
56 Not working
58 Sax range
59 Lettuce unit
60 Norway's capital
62 Fourth-yr. students
64 Wing of a building

ure
38 Dots in the ocean (abbr.)
40 Common teen affliction
43 Question from one friend to another upon seeing a stranger
46 Too
47 "___ Lay Dying" (Faulkner novel)
49 Not obvious at all
51 Like fishnets
52 Lag behind
53 Elevate
54 Henry VIII's house, represented by a rose
55 Important atmospheric constituent
56 Trip plotting
57 "Sad to say ..."
60 Top-notch
61 Former German capital
62 Card game with a name that sounds like a command to a pesky cat
64 Until now
66 Higher power, for many

For Our Neighbors to the North

by Boris Loring

Copyright © Devarai GmbH

ACROSS

1 Wild swine
5 Slitherers along the Nile
9 Trophy or ribbon, maybe
14 Church area that sounds like iPhone downloadables
15 Hic, ___, hoc (Latin I declension)
16 The "Caveman" diet
17 Nancy Reagan's simplistic solution to drug abuse
19 Wipe out
20 The Jetsons' dog
21 Retail promotion
23 Managed care gps.
24 Truman Capote's 1966 novel about a notorious Kansas murder
27 Hard Italian cheese
30 "You've Got Mail" ISP
31 Laze
32 Anne who lost her head to Henry VIII
36 Le ___-Soleil (Louis XIV's sobriquet)
39 Oklahoma's second largest city
41 Was victorious
42 Furry denizens of Endor's forest, in the "Star Wars" franchise
44 Word that can follow "special" or "photo"
45 Largest country in North America, whose current prime minister can be found by pronouncing the first words of 17-, 24-, 52-, and 65-Across
48 Precipitation whose size is often compared to golf balls
49 Comedy skit show with a Weekend Update, for short
50 Ooey-gooey campfire treats
52 Books such as 24-Across
57 Like much of North Africa and the Middle East
58 Anise-flavored Greek aperitif
59 Uses a dagger
63 Members of the flock
65 Curved mixer attachment used for making bread
67 Alternative to the middle or window, on an airplane
68 "Hang ___ your hat!"
69 "Downton Abbey" lady's maid beset by all sorts of trials and tribulations
70 Wet, wintry weather mixture
71 Clarinet, e.g.
72 Striped circus covering

DOWN

1 Western Mexico peninsula
2 Magnum ___ (great artistic work)
3 Aide (abbr.)
4 Courtroom do overs
5 "Eureka!"
6 Authority
7 Type of code or colony
8 Reprimand
9 Creature with "stinking paws," in a Charlton Heston sci-fi movie
10 Artist know for his Marilyn Monroe series
11 1836 Texas battle site
12 Repair a bare spot in a lawn, perhaps
13 Stags' mates
18 Ditty
22 Online auction site
25 Detritus from eating an ear of corn
26 Sole
27 Voice range that means "high"
28 Vichyssoise or borscht
29 Woes
33 Possess
34 Mauna ___
35 Finale
36 Holler like a lion
37 Dust Bowl fig-

choice
66 Ruckus

Building Harmony

by Patrick Merrell

Copyright © Devarai GmbH

ACROSS

1 Glance over
5 Rudimentary
10 Sci-fi sky sightings
14 Wee
15 Whatsoever
16 Sweat source
17 Recuperation
18 Martini's vermouth-making partner
19 Enormous
20 Song for a would-be builder?
23 Flanders in "The Simpsons"
24 Leaking-balloon letters in a comic strip
25 Potato-sack material
28 Like the gods Athena and Zeus
30 Pull, using a truck
33 Honkers in a flock
34 Suffix with gang, in rap lingo
36 Low-down polish site
38 Detective's case-solving cry
39 Song for a builder (or satellite dish installer)?
43 Chewie's chum
45 Japanese Prime Minister Shinzo ___
46 HDTV maker
47 Book of photos
50 Artist known as Jean in France and Hans in Germany
52 Blow, as Krakatoa did in 1883
56 Health club hot boxes
58 Gran or bran add-on
60 Take to court
61 Singing duo who sound like builders?
65 Western mil. alliance
67 From Korea or Vietnam
68 Threw ___ (blew a gasket)
69 False god
70 Copy, for short
71 Debussy's "Claire de ___"
72 Like a skeleton
73 Observes Ramadan
74 Dressed

DOWN

1 Kite flyer's ball
2 Donald Sutherland's son
3 Not outdoors
4 Old wives' tale
5 Medieval poets
6 "I'd like to propose ___"
7 Diagonally worn piece of royal regalia
8 Ingrid's "Casablanca" role
9 Scale, as a mountain
10 "Hey, I'm right above you"
11 Lucky kind of clover
12 Nonprofit's website ending
13 "Told you so!"
21 Invite as one's date for
22 One-fisted piece of barware
26 Pale wood
27 Thick-soup ingredient
29 Seer's gift, for short
31 "None of the above" category
32 Anguish
35 "Gimme ___!" (part of an Alabama cheer)
37 Foul up
39 Start to take off a dress shirt
40 Not-yet-set abbr.
41 Most of the earth's surface
42 Rowboat accessory
43 Owns
44 Pie ___ mode
48 Wicked
49 West known for her one-liners
51 Andy Warhol specialty
53 Handy
54 Puppy Chow packager
55 Ran up the flagpole
57 Snowman's neckwear
59 "Jay ___ Garage" (TV show)
62 Sailing towards Europe, e.g.
63 Tears apart
64 Soft mineral
65 Speedball pen

"Stock Options"

by Kelly Clark

Copyright © Devarai GmbH

ACROSS

1 Salinger heroine
5 Log home
10 Blue hue
14 Neighbor of Vietnam
15 Japanese verse
16 Pink, as a steak
17 Buy, buy, buy environment
19 Just makes, with "out"
20 Poem of praise
21 Soothing succulent
22 Say again
24 The Magi, e.g.
26 ___ mignon (tender steak)
27 Lard, say
28 Sneeze response
31 Takes it easy
34 Pilotless plane
35 Yang's counterpart
36 Word of woe
37 "Beauty and the ___"
38 Sentry's cry
39 Peacock network
40 King protectors, in chess
41 Japan's capital
42 Thrown off the train track
44 Spigot
45 English class assignment
46 50-50 chances
50 Highway divider
52 Executive attire, often
53 Dine
54 Killer whale
55 Open audition...or this puzzle's theme?
58 King of the jungle
59 Fill with joy
60 Aptly named citrus fruit
61 Morning moistures
62 Bank account subtraction
63 Superlatively good

DOWN

1 Macaroni shape
2 Mecca resident
3 Secret agents
4 Immigrant's class: Abbr.
5 Alpine house
6 Composer Copland
7 Two-wheeled transport
8 Eisenhower's nickname
9 Vitamin, e.g.
10 Thin pancakes
11 Talk, talk, talk
12 Carpet layer's calculation
13 Hatchling's home
18 Papas' mates
23 "If all ___ fails ..."
25 Young newts
26 Dentist's advice
28 Trade name
29 Too smooth
30 Golden Rule word
31 "Atlas Shrugged" author Ayn
32 Hamburg's river
33 It's above criticism, facetiously
34 Library decimal system inventor
37 Like a healthy diet
38 Emulates a bunny
40 City with a leaning tower
41 One of the senses
43 Koreans, e.g.
44 Bathroom fixture
46 ___-frutti
47 Grammar topic
48 Tugs
49 Bowling challenge
50 Shape, as character
51 Pennsylvania port
52 Knife wound
56 Drink in a mug
57 Bear's baby

59 ___ Men ("Who Let the Dogs Out?" band)
60 Barely made, with "out"
61 Work at a bar
63 Holster filler
64 U.F.O. drivers
65 Go bad

The Two-in-One Zoo

by Patrick Merrell

Copyright © Devarai GmbH

ACROSS

1 Not-yet-set abbr.
4 Nurse, as a drink
7 Film studio with a roaring lion logo
10 "Terrif!"
13 One of 100 electees on Capitol Hill
15 "My lips ___ sealed"
16 Distinct time period
17 Small desert hopper
19 Eggy winter drink
20 Make "grr!" sounds
21 Confession admission
22 Mail order store for Wile E. Coyote
23 Large land and (mostly) sea mammal
27 Regains consciousness
30 Talk incessantly
31 Still in the bunk
32 Under the effects of Novocain
35 Network that covers the U.S. Congress
39 Day after the weekend, on a cal.
40 Swimmer with taste buds on its whiskers
42 Angsty music genre
43 Pitcher Martinez
45 When tripled, blah, blah, blah
46 Big hairdos, for short
47 Once-while connector
49 Mandatory language for airline pilots
51 Treetop swinger whose tail is longer than its body
56 Flapping superhero garb
57 Little Red Book leader
58 Dalai Lama's land
62 In the style of
63 Non-venomous rattler lookalike
66 Apt. parts
67 Online address letters
68 Make more difficult, with "up"
69 Zigzagging road section
70 Bill, the Science Guy
71 Longtime car racing sponsor
72 Tack on

DOWN

1 Sounds of disapproval
2 Word after navy, black or jelly
3 Tennis's Kournikova
4 Horse barn divisions
5 Suffix with super
6 Not amateur
7 "West Side Story" heroine
8 ___ Smith apples
9 Attained, as a goal
10 Outdoor wall
11 Enticing smell
12 Roll with a hole
14 "Deal!"
18 ___Kosh B'Gosh
22 Verbalizes one's curiosity
24 Famed Sicilian mountain
25 Looking displeased
26 RPM dial
27 Kid's summer getaway
28 Clarinet relative
29 Fix, as a tear
33 Graphic designer's graduate deg.
34 Obama's V.P.
36 Prefix with scope
37 "Famous" cookie maker
38 Quick bite
40 Edible scoop holder
41 Ended up on the seafloor
44 Amusement park attraction
46 Taking a helicopter
48 Weapons storehouse
50 Rises, from being knocked down
51 Frighten
52 They reveal all to some fortune tellers
53 "That's not for me, thanks"
54 Type of leaf on Canada's flag
55 Sound of intrigue

Initial Impressions

by Elizabeth C. Gorski

Copyright © Devarai GmbH

ACROSS

1 Little demons
5 Tortilla chip topped with cheese
10 Jell-O shaper
14 Tidy
15 Ambulance alert
16 Tied in score
17 Ottawa
20 Retired Oldsmobile model
21 Perfume compounds
22 Estonia, once (Abbr.)
23 Probability
25 Bar bills
28 ___ Alto, Calif.
30 School in E. Lansing
32 One-time connection
34 Far from fetching
36 Boarding house occupant
39 ___ Aviv
40 Contents of a travel bag
43 Back muscle, in gym-speak
44 Use a fondue fork
45 Norway's largest city
46 Chemical suffix
47 USO audience
48 Farmer's harvest
50 Regarding
52 Choir voice
54 Where surgeons work (Abbr.)
57 Plaza Hotel heroine of kiddie lit
60 "Haystacks" painter
62 Generous gift for a bubbly lover
66 Last writes?
67 "___ cold, starve a fever"
68 Dickens no goodnik
69 Obama predecessor
70 Knapsack part
71 Exploits

DOWN

1 Peruvians of yore
2 Breakfast, lunch and dinner
3 Floppy disks at a picnic?
4 Use a swizzle stick
5 Code-breaking org.
6 Had the flu
7 Christian symbol
8 Weightiness
9 "___ upon a time ..."
10 High-IQ group
11 Lab eggs
12 Conducted
13 "CSI" evidence
18 Hammer or wrench
19 Maestro Toscanini
24 Start of the musical scale
26 Loofahs and such
27 "Stainless" fork material
29 "The Fountainhead" author Rand
30 2150, to Cato
31 Choose
33 Furthermore
34 Bruins' sch.
35 West African nation
37 "Clumsy me!"
38 One ___ kind (unique)
41 Paid male escort
42 As well
49 Cavort
51 Dentist's expertise
52 One of the 12 tribes of Israel
53 "You can ___ horse to ..."
55 Actress Zellweger
56 Staircase units
58 Switch settings
59 "Rhyme Pays" rapper
61 Honolulu's isle
62 Corn throwaway
63 ___ Dhabi
64 Bro's sib
65 Tourist's need

51 Story line
52 Simple
53 Toy dog with a flat face
54 Japanese Prime Minister Shinzo
55 Response to the question, "Do you take this person to be your lawful wedded spouse?"
56 Take a load off

Fourth Down and Ten

by Boris Loring

Copyright © Devarai GmbH

ACROSS

1 Signal to an auctioneer
4 Fist ___ (casual greetings)
9 Ford flop of the 1950s
14 What a tree's rings indicate
15 Bygone Apple laptop
16 Like melted cheese
17 Be feverish
20 Oakland athlete
21 More broad
22 Column to the right of the tens
23 Agenda bullet points
25 Secretive govt. org. for which Edward Snowden worked
28 Lump of gum
29 Devotional sites
31 Debt acknowledgments
32 Oily film
33 Tosses the first chips into the poker pot
34 Cash in one's chips
38 Wacky craze
39 Seeps
40 Waiflike Kate on the cover of many a British Vogue
41 Open and honest
43 Rodent with a bad reputation
46 Suffix for Vietnam and Japan, but not Laos or Thailand
47 Shrewd
48 Place to have a bite in Paris ... or the drink you might order there
49 Solo
51 Magazine with a "Sexiest Man Alive" issue
53 What Congress can do when there isn't gridlock
57 WWII German sub
58 "See ya later, amigo"
59 Prosecutors (abbr.)
60 Ladies and ___
61 Toilet, in kidspeak
62 Pig's digs

DOWN

1 The "Clyde" of Bonnie & Clyde
2 Belizean's "tree chicken"
3 Refused, as a bank loan
4 Chomp down on
5 Company that has caused the value of a taxi medallion to plummet
6 With 7-Down, the metaphorical owners of a small business
7 See 6-Down
8 Shish kebab spike
9 "Zounds!"
10 Lavish affection (on)
11 Unpleasant interruption in an otherwise agreeable situation
12 Suffix for mountain or profit
13 Basic cleaner
18 Classified section's listings
19 Wheel parts
23 It makes you scratch
24 Call on a movie set
26 Fat in many a classic English pudding
27 Total jerk
29 ___-Seltzer
30 Illuminated
31 Tattoo artist's array
32 Bio. and Chem., e.g.
33 Sailed through with flying colors
34 CONTROL's nemesis on "Get Smart"
35 Like oysters in months containing the letter "R"
36 Corpse
37 Israeli submachine gun
38 Marseilles Mrs.
41 Walking stick's kin
42 Hallmark of a May-December romance
43 Kayaker's white water challenge
44 Buoyant
45 Itty-bitty
47 Team that moved from Baltimore to Indianapolis
48 Barracks bed
50 Aspiring attorney's graduate entrance exam (abbr.)

chain with a syrup line

57 Prefix meaning "bone"

58 "This is ___ for Superman!"

60 Funnywoman Bombeck

62 Restroom sign

63 Autograph seeker

Devarai CROSSWORDS

Puzzle 31
www.devarai.com

Presidential Places

by Patrick Merrell

Copyright © Devarai GmbH

ACROSS

1 Four-wheeler on a par 3
5 Code inventor of fame
10 Sometimes paid-for newspaper bio
14 "Zip-___-Doo Dah"
15 Constellation with a three star "belt"
16 Bond villain with a guano mine on Crab Key
17 U.S. president whose middle and last names are both Massachusetts towns
20 Seventh planet from the Sun
21 32-card game
22 Good or hood suffix
23 State whose capital is Lincoln (abbr.)
24 "So that's what you mean"
26 Possess
28 Included in on an email, briefly
29 Was against
33 Silverman or Palin
36 "This ___ joke!"
38 Prefix meaning "eight"
39 U.S. president whose last name is a city on Lake Erie
42 Rideable, as a horse
43 "Back ___!" ("Same here!")
44 Dunham and Horne
45 Doesn't eat for a long time
47 Scot's family
49 Direction a SSW wind blows
50 Short start of a long journey
51 "You've got mail" co.
54 Commandment no-no
56 Tin can eater in cartoons
59 Winged African biter
61 U.S. president with more than a dozen towns named after him
64 Come in last
65 Pitch-related, in music
66 Not spicy
67 "___ Sesame!"
68 Black wood used for oboes and pianos
69 Splitters that are swung

DOWN

1 Spicy New Orleans cuisine
2 Love to bits
3 Detox locale
4 Nashville's state (abbr.)
5 Fluffy chocolate bowlful
6 "Do it ___ quit!"
7 Second instruction on a shampoo bottle
8 Dresser item used as a puppet
9 One-named Irish singer
10 Peculiar
11 Head shot, so to speak
12 "You've Got a Friend ___"
13 Mix, as a salad
18 Brunch pie
19 Sitting on
25 Imperial decrees
27 Like many mittens and caps
28 Stalactite site
29 Like a short play
30 Movie angle (inits.)
31 Sicilian mountain
32 Ones given cards and, often, ties in June
33 Barracks barkers (abbr.)
34 "I smell ___" ("Something's fishy")
35 Facial feature with a prominent bridge
37 Crafty
40 Singer Corinne Bailey
41 Tick by, as time
46 Lyra's brightest star
48 Unloose, as a Frisbee
50 ___ pad (reporter's notebook)
51 When an early dinner might be served
52 "___ Mio"
53 Gives temporarily
54 D-Day French city
55 Restaurant

Age-Appropriate Fun

by Elizabeth C. Gorski

Copyright © Devarai GmbH

ACROSS

1 Rocker Clapton
5 Be unselfish
10 Rewards for waiters
14 Mexican snack in a shell
15 Young assistants in the Senate
16 Operatic solo
17 Plum, peach, or cherry, e.g.
19 Put up, as curtains
20 Streisand film of 1983
21 "Wee" boy
22 Saturn surrounders
23 Ireland
25 Braille marking
26 Third-place winner at the Olympics
33 Wildlife identifier
34 Staffer
35 Improved partner?
37 No ifs, ___, or buts
38 NASCAR advertiser
39 Yellow cab
40 JFK's predecessor
41 Honolulu's island
43 Unprincipled
45 Dietary extra that may treat anemia
48 Sales agent, for short
49 Actor Alan
50 Low-sounding marching band instruments
53 Bygone jet
55 Start of a wishful statement
59 Ms. Brockovich
60 Ditsy person
62 Awestruck
63 Should, with "to"
64 Opposite of east
65 Not as expensive
66 Uses a rosary, say
67 "Titanic" actress Winslet

DOWN

1 Online marketplace for handmade goods
2 Hotel room cost
3 Desktop trash can, e.g.
4 Table of ___ (book's front matter)
5 Tanning-lotion letters
6 Section of Manhattan that's north of Central Park
7 Spanish for "water"
8 "American Pie" actress Tara
9 Repairman's fig.
10 South Pacific vacation mecca
11 Persia, today
12 Submarine sonar sound
13 Droops
18 "My Fair Lady" heroine
22 Actor's quest
24 Rule, for short
25 Mom's mate
26 Abacus slider
27 The Amazing ___ (magician)
28 Select from a menu
29 Consume with gusto
30 Quick swim
31 Entrap
32 Dallas dweller
36 Droop
38 Moo ___ pork
39 Weapon you might see in a Native American museum
41 Change for a five-dollar bill
42 Nile snake
43 100%
44 Army doc
46 Borneo swingers, briefly
47 Inconsistent
50 Greenish-blue duck
51 Desire
52 Some book jacket blurbs
53 Cowboy boot feature
54 It's a long story
56 Classic theaters
57 Annoying person
58 Diminutive suffix
60 Soak (up)
61 UFO crew

My BA-add!

by Elizabeth C. Gorski

Copyright © Devarai GmbH

ACROSS

1 Competent
5 Social no-nos
11 Cartoon frame
14 Jellystone Park's Yogi ___
15 Stern and Newton
16 St. crosser
17 Storybook elephant's PowerPoint diagrams?
19 Queen in a hive
20 Rene of "Ransom"
21 Old U.S. gas brand
22 Flirtatious blink of an eye
23 "Evil Woman" band
25 Emulates Monet
27 Lethal washbowls?
33 Barn bird
34 Faction
35 Hoodlums
39 Long jumps
42 "Caught ya!"
43 Neighbor of Iraq
44 "Law & Order" proceeding
45 Like a marshmallow
47 ___ Lanka
48 Wine made by actress Lauren?
52 The "T" of a BLT
55 Toothpaste-approving org.
56 Egyptian goddess
57 Modest skirt length
61 "West Side Story" character
65 Skillet
66 Pastry chef with a golden touch?
68 Pvt.'s superior
69 Lack of vitality
70 Slender bottle part
71 "Of course"
72 Wedding reception highlights
73 Chows down

DOWN

1 Shortened wd.
2 Boyfriend
3 Scientists' workplaces
4 Deleted
5 Twitch
6 Tennis legend Arthur
7 Sheep-ish cries
8 Sticks in the water?
9 Eight-armed sea creatures
10 Snake's warning
11 Rustic home
12 Occurrence
13 Onion relatives
18 Hot dog holder
22 ___-washy
24 Exclamations of woe
26 Tiny picnic crashers
27 Nitwit
28 Ornamental jug
29 Jai ___
30 "Beauty and the ___"
31 Sneeze sound
32 Office crew
36 Bear of the night sky
37 Lass
38 Go yachting
40 Mamas' mates
41 Opening for a coin
46 TV schedule abbr.
49 Sharp Italian cheese
50 First man?
51 Conical tooth
52 Slightly drunk
53 River of Missouri
54 After-dinner candies
58 Swedish furniture chain
59 Turns down the lights
60 "What's ___ for me?"
62 Notion
63 Diplomat's skill
64 Requests
66 Vampire's alter ego
67 Cooking fuel

57 Tied up in ___
58 Probably the only chair designer you've ever heard of
62 Beer ingredient
63 Leaf-raker's creation
64 Boatload
66 Abbr. after Lexington, on a Manhattan street sign
68 Astound
69 Affirmative "Are you?" response

Rhyme Time

by Patrick Merrell

Copyright © Devarai GmbH

ACROSS

1 Lugosi of "Dracula"
5 Mary had a little one
9 "Burnt" paint color
14 Myth or method suffix
15 Only U.S. state with a non-rectangular flag
16 Home of the Dolphins
17 Ranter's remedy
19 Player that moves second in chess
20 "Ditto for me"
21 In the vicinity
23 Extra-wide shoe letters
24 Minor traffic mishap
28 Boxer born Cassius Clay
31 ___ Paolo, Brazil
32 Norwegian capital
33 Aching body part, often
35 Use a Lawn Boy
37 Highest-ranking asst. at the state level
41 Monster movie
45 Goat-legged Greek diety
46 Curtsy's counterpart
47 Sign of things to come
48 Fireworks reactions, perhaps
51 "That's amazing!"
53 Leprechaun's gold holder
54 Kid's communication toy
59 Judge in the O.J. trial
60 Unauthorized disclosure
61 Electrical items with shades
65 N.F.L. player since 2016 (after the team returned from St. Louis)
67 Stamped correspondence
70 Rome's ___ Fountain
71 "Field of Dreams" state
72 Magazine title that translates to "she"
73 Vicks decongestant spray
74 Stern's opposite, on a ship
75 Meat and vegetable dish

DOWN

1 Cheap pens or lighters
2 "Hello ... hello ... hello," for example
3 Put down, as macadam
4 ___ the above (everything)
5 Cut (off)
6 Yellowfin tuna, on menus
7 A.A. who created Pooh and Roo
8 Ravel work featured in the movie "10"
9 Rainy day pop up
10 Trash bag thickness unit
11 Sounded sheepish?
12 Dais introducer
13 Picard's second-in-command on the starship Enterprise
18 What solemn oaths prevent, in theory
22 Rock-hard muscles, for short
25 Killer whale in a film title
26 Hinged one in a hallway
27 "___ dwell on the subject, but ..."
28 Basic info
29 Dr. Zhivago's love
30 Rapper whose name sounds like a drink
34 Craft with a two-bladed oar
36 Fly catcher in a deserted house
38 "Forrest ___"
39 Cookie in cookies and cream, often
40 Hot-air discharger
42 Hiker's snack
43 Chicken or turkey
44 Teddy bear like fighter on the planet Endor
49 Doubled, a giggle
50 Equilibrium
52 Last ___ and testament
54 Loses crispness, as lettuce
55 Pong maker
56 '60s sex symbol Sophia

Always and Forever

by Elizabeth C. Gorski

Copyright © Devarai GmbH

ACROSS

1 "___ Abby" (advice column)
5 Turkey-stuffing herb
9 "Seize the Day" author Bellow
13 Otherwise
14 Hawaiian greeting
15 Farmland unit
16 Severely harm
17 Hindu princesses
18 Actress Russo
19 "Timeless" David Foster Wallace novel of 1996
22 Doze (off)
23 Run at full speed
27 Oodles
30 Mac alternatives
33 Subscribe again
34 Big, heavy book
35 Tropical rum cocktail
37 Italian "three"
38 "Timeless" Gloria Estefan hit of 1995
41 Slithery fish
42 Summer office worker
43 Work without ___ (take risks)
44 Light refractor
46 TV spots
47 Sanctify
48 Irritating radio noise
50 Birds ___ feather
51 "Timeless" hit song by the Bangles
58 OktoberFest drink
61 Of sound mind
62 Ant contingent
63 Leer at
64 Russian rulers
65 "Scream" actress Campbell
66 Virtuoso cellist ___ Ma
67 Salty septet
68 Orator's platform

DOWN

1 "G.I. Jane" portrayer Moore
2 Flair
3 "Dream on!"
4 Online calendar pop-up
5 Venetian blind part
6 Top-notch
7 Quartet before K
8 Relaxes
9 "No Exit" playwright Jean Paul
10 Untouchable tennis serve
11 Samovar
12 Actor Tommy ___ Jones
14 Bone-dry
20 Refusals
21 Parsley piece
24 Chant
25 The jitters
26 Messages from President Trump
27 Brews, as tea
28 Secret, like a CIA operation
29 Aviator Earhart
30 Ziti or rigatoni
31 Gave as an example
32 Uses a swizzle stick
35 Chess piece
36 Raggedy doll
39 Maximum
40 Dreamy state, or the title of a 2016 film
45 Sound investment for a den?
47 Texter's closest buddy
49 Boston hoopsters, for short
50 Early automaker
52 Sneaky plan
53 March Madness gp.
54 Broadcasts
55 Length x width
56 2006, on a cornerstone
57 Seeing things?
58 Lad
59 Swelled head
60 TV Tarzan Ron

Suffix Rethink

by Patrick Merrell

Copyright © Devarai GmbH

ACROSS

1 Titanic sinker, for short
5 Sound booster at a concert
8 Frisbee company
13 Egg-shaped
14 Put into words
16 One of more than 7.5 billion on Earth
17 Mobile communication device of the '80s, in comparison to today's?
19 Chilling, as champagne
20 Sacha Baron Cohen movie after "Borat"
21 They make calls at home
23 Moo ___ pork
24 Winning boat in the America's Cup race?
28 Graceful antelope
31 Oahu souvenir
32 Within
33 Mushroom part
36 Dentistry photos
40 Buddhism branch
41 Tiny insect that's gotten into the fridge?
43 No vote
44 Halo-headed one
46 Gumbo vegetable
47 Fixtures filled with 20s, briefly
48 Harbor boat
50 Salon worker
52 Wifeless gang member?
57 Toothpaste tube letters
58 Gold strike
59 Joltless joe
63 One summoned by rubbing
65 Number for a ward of the state?
68 Fake-eyeball material
69 Disrespectful
70 Gait between walk and canter
71 Cheerleading calls
72 Where many G.I.'s served in the '60s
73 Border

DOWN

1 Box office failure
2 At any time
3 Robusto! sauce maker
4 Took a brief look
5 What charcoal turns into
6 Chinese chairman
7 Put on a bulletin board
8 Busy deli worker's question
9 Attila, for one
10 Folks in the movie "Witness"
11 The speed of sound
12 Outdo
15 Moore or Lovato
18 "Gateway" author Frederik
22 D.C. dealmaker
25 In addition
26 "Likewise"
27 Dubbed man
28 Israel's ___ Strip
29 Prayer-ending word
30 Zip
34 Antlered animal that bugles
35 Bog
37 One opposed
38 Orange tubers
39 The "S" in CBS (abbr.)
41 Totally out of it
42 Grp. with peacekeeping forces
45 Do or say follower in the Bible
47 Firm, as pasta
49 Day-___ paint
51 Knee-high Jedi
52 Like oversized pants
53 "19" and "21" singer
54 Isthmus of Panama crosser
55 Olfactory input
56 Episode that's aired before
60 Businessman's handout
61 Slack-jawed
62 Wingding
64 Martha's Vineyard or Nantucket (abbr.)
66 High-tech appt. book
67 Skirt's bottom

50 Uses the rubber end of a pencil

52 Grammarian's concern

53 Southeast Asia's ___ Peninsula

55 Bedside rouser

57 Mexican temple builder

59 Fail's opposite

60 "Garfield" dog

61 Fava or pinto

62 New Rochelle, NY, college

63 TV series featuring a plane crash on a mysterious island

67 Prefix with functional

But They're Not Capital Cities

by Patrick Merrell

Copyright © Devarai GmbH

ACROSS

1 Go off script
6 Run away
10 Recipe meas.
14 John ___ tractors
15 Neeson in three "Taken" movies
16 Accumulation on a barber shop floor
17 Omar Khayyam: "___ of bread, a jug of wine, and thou"
18 Prefix with dynamic
19 First word of many fairy tales
20 The most populous city in Europe, discounting that half of it is in Asia
23 "Eldorado" rock gp.
24 "You bet!"
25 Legally protected images (abbr.)
26 Ultimate degree
29 It's checked off while shopping
32 Item worn by Mickey Mouse but not Donald Duck
34 Greek love god
36 "Your Majesty" alternative
38 DeGeneres of daytime TV
41 The most populous city on the smallest continent
44 Add in as an extra
45 Plateau that drops off on all sides
46 Desires
47 Furry little warrior in "Return of the Jedi"
49 Arena topper
51 Q followers
52 "Yer out!" caller
54 Mauna ___ (the world's largest above ground volcano)
56 Division such as the Paleozoic
58 The most populous city in the Southern or Western Hemisphere
64 Alan of "M*A*S*H"
65 Lessen in color
66 Responded to a cry of "All rise!"
68 Comic bits
69 Operatic solo
70 Wee
71 People can cross, close, and roll them
72 Marvel mutants
73 Sings using nonsense syllables

DOWN

1 Toothpaste-approving org.
2 Store that slices to order
3 Late-July babies
4 Really angry
5 Happen to
6 Extra inches around the waist
7 In ___ of (instead of)
8 Like birds that get worms
9 Doesn't hide one's feelings, on stage
10 Superhero named for a Norse god
11 Human equivalent of an ATM
12 Command to an attack dog
13 Hunts, with "on"
21 Like garbage trucks, when you're trying to sleep
22 Aisle-walking employee
26 Egg-hatching spot, often
27 "___ Little Tenderness"
28 Mishmash
30 Thailand, once
31 Realigned, as a wheel
33 Skin care brand
35 Wintertime precipitation
37 Canadian gas brand
39 One, for Angela Merkel
40 Cartoonist Thomas who fashioned the present-day Santa
42 ___ Gay (W.W. II bomber)
43 Less wild
48 American pitching great Sandy

leave it as it is]

52 After-dinner candy

55 Skirt's edging

56 "___ Baba and the Forty Thieves"

57 Baton Rouge sch.

58 What a cow chews on

59 "Listen up!"

"Bible Jeopardy: Noah by the Numbers!"

by Kelly Clark

Copyright © Devarai GmbH

ACROSS

1 Pitch
6 Double-reed instruments
11 Like some dry humor
14 Kind of salad dressing
15 Flip (out)
16 Ground breaking tool?
17 The number of days and nights of the Great Flood.: 3 wds.
19 Physicians' org.
20 Scatter
21 Carafe size
23 U-turn from ENE
26 Corn serving, at a cookout
27 Paperback, versus hardcover, e.g.
29 Capital of Greece
31 Biases
32 Sounds like a lion
33 The "hard stuff"
34 Pitching star
37 Young 'uns
38 Big name in baseball trading cards
39 Luxurious bathroom features
40 U.S. Star Wars letters, in the Reagan era
41 Smooth transition
42 Flies, big time
43 Close tightly: 2 wds.
45 At the scene: hyph.
46 Colors a tee shirt, hippie style: hyph.
48 Classic dessert
49 Latin king?
50 Out of whack
51 House of the Seven Gables Massachusetts city
53 Fall behind
54 Number of fleas Noah's dog wanted to enter the ark.: 3 wds.(Okay, I made this one up)
60 "___ bin ein Berliner"
61 She had "the face that launched a thousand ships"
62 Follow as a result
63 Halifax clock setting: Abbr.
64 Leaves out
65 Prepare for an exam

DOWN

1 Old credit-reporting company, initially
2 "What a joke!"
3 Genetic info carrier, briefly
4 Halloween mos.
5 Bleaches, maybe
6 Proposal
7 Arch over the eye
8 "Star-Spangled Banner" preposition
9 Have a bite
10 Notable New York City view
11 So-so poker hand...and the set of animals who entered the ark.: 4 wds.
12 Juliet's love
13 Ache (for)
18 Sp. married ladies
22 "The Addams Family" cousin
23 Witches' facial features
24 Got up
25 The number of people who escaped the Great Flood.: 3 wds.
27 Wed on the run
28 Haagen-___ ice cream
30 Hospital trauma areas, briefly
31 Absorb, as gravy with a slice of bread: 2 wds.
33 Fake
35 ___ blanche
36 Colchester's county
38 Prefix with marketing
39 Brillo rival
41 "And the source of your claim is?": 2 wds.
42 Cold sufferers' elicits for blessings?
44 Actors Asner and Begley
45 Lubricates
46 Actress Shire of the "Rocky" movies
47 Apple computers
48 Aches
51 [Never mind,

cpls.
56 "Eww!"
57 Aerosol container
58 Despot Amin
59 1/7 of a week
60 Caribbean ___
61 Wriggly swimmer
62 JFK's predecessor

Alternate Meanings

by Patrick Merrell

Copyright © Devarai GmbH

ACROSS

1 Coconut-bearing tree
5 Great white relative
9 Reprimand
14 Epps or Khayyám
15 Previously owned
16 Matt of "Today"
17 "After saying her vows, the bride was ..."
19 Chunnel change, perhaps
20 Words that start a back pedaling explanation
21 A smoker might bum one
22 Partin' words
25 "During the blackout, everyone in town was ..."
30 Becomes involved with, as an enemy
32 Place to park your butt
33 Entered, as in a ship's record
34 Invoice fig.
35 You ___ here
36 "For violating the club rules, the man was ..."
40 Tax-filing mo.
42 Suffix with adult
43 Repairs the bottom of a skirt
46 One making casual drawings
49 Canada's most populous province
50 "Once the tight deadline passed, she felt ..."
52 Burning crime
53 Half of a couple
54 Jeans material
56 Cake covering
59 "At the grand opening, the store's entrance was ..."
63 U.S. Military Academy student
64 Additionally
65 Necessity
66 Jewish potato turnover
67 Supporting votes in the House
68 Harvard rival

DOWN

1 Pea holder
2 "Me, really?"
3 Notes to follow "so"
4 Daniel-san's mentor in "The Karate Kid"
5 Poet's inspiration
6 Syrian ruling family
7 Pen name for the many Nancy Drew writers, Carolyn ___
8 Not even
9 Santa's transportation
10 Nabbed
11 Notre Dame = ___ Lady
12 Astrological lion
13 Medical practitioners (abbr.)
18 Mental pictures
21 Underground reservoir for rainwater
22 Salt, in France
23 Ambient musician Brian
24 Kind of Chinese soup
26 Young sheep
27 Stock exchange workers
28 Word before drum or phone
29 Change the color of
31 Republican attorney general whose name is spelled using only the letters in DEMS
34 Comedian Schumer or Poehler
37 Messes up
38 Price that's marked up from wholesale
39 Online dating company with an 80-year-old spokesman
40 Put numbers together
41 "The Raven"author
44 "O Sole ___"
45 Kiefer Sutherland, to Donald
47 Goes on and on and on
48 Measurement from stem to stern
49 Ukraine's largest seaport
51 Roman official that's an anagram of "elide"
55 Sgts. and

50 Like food blessed by the rabbi
53 Had dinner at home
54 Swap
56 Drug that's the subject of the movie "Awakenings"
57 Like some seals and pitchers
58 100,000 of them are in a newton
60 Docile
61 Slush Puppie relative
62 Band's booking
63 "Green" prefix for tourism or terrorism

Devarai CROSSWORDS

Puzzle 40

www.devarai.com

The Green Party?

by Boris Loring

Copyright © Devarai GmbH

ACROSS

1 Rowboater's need
5 Breathe like an excited dog
9 Cruise line's shore offerings
14 Response to a fresh remark, perhaps
15 Baseball's Moises, Felipe, Jesús or Matty
16 Saturn and Mercury, but not Earth
17 Athletic shoe brand whose logo includes an upward arrow
18 Astronomer Sagan of "Cosmos" fame
19 Bitewings and mammograms
20 March 17th lapel button worn by those from the Old Sod, maybe
23 Having iron poor blood
24 What some houses are built on
25 Neptune's domain
28 Hunk of bacon
30 Linguini, ziti, and orecchiette
32 Internet domain letters used by many non-profit groups
35 Anglicized version of a Gaelic phrase expressing loyalty to the Old Sod
38 "Répondez s'il ___ plaît"
40 Gunky stuff
41 Suit to ___
42 Colorful name for the Old Sod, with "the"
47 Ambulance destinations, for short
48 Live (in)
49 Warmonger
51 Tyke
52 First-year med school subj.
55 Like ornately decorated leather
59 Mid-March celebration for those with Old Sod roots
62 Imply
64 Apop
65 Honker
66 Start of a Caesarean boast
67 ___ fixe
68 Fencer's blade
69 Like some badly injured matadors
70 Require
71 Dosage units for 19-Across

DOWN

1 Honshu seaport with a 16th century castle
2 Theodore and Simon's chipmunk colleague
3 It might accompany a promotion
4 Muscle contractions
5 Leader of an Indy 500 warm-up
6 Jai ___
7 Standards
8 Flower from Holland
9 Many a yellow vehicle on a New York City street
10 Yours and mine
11 The Aggies of the NCAA Mountain West Conference
12 Former Alabama judge Moore who lost a hotly contested 2017 election
13 Draft board agcy.
21 5,280 feet
22 Car once owned by a deadbeat, maybe
26 Like a clichéd beaver
27 Fireplace debris
29 Dallas's nickname
31 Mme in Madrid
32 Blatant
33 Loverboy
34 Bob Newhart on "The Big Bang Theory," e.g.
36 "There's ___ in 'team'"
37 "Golly!"
39 ___ Lanka
43 Engaged in a bit of evolution
44 Dunham of "Girls"
45 Securely fastened
46 Cuddly-looking "Star Wars" creature

54 Festive party
55 Cheese named for a Dutch town
56 Detective Nancy of kid lit
60 "Xanadu" band, for short
61 Sphere

Third Rock

by Boris Loring

Copyright © Devarai GmbH

ACROSS

1 Prominent feature of the Capitol
5 Space-age tool used by some surgeons
10 Sport with ponies
14 "Stop!," in pony-speak
15 Stubborn as ___
16 Route
17 Mother Nature's soil aerators
19 Church part that sounds like smartphone downloadables
20 Pitcher's stat
21 Brontë heroine Jane
22 No-tell motel rendezvous
24 San Francisco and vicinity
26 Landed
27 Mark Spitz set seven of them at the 1972 Olympics
32 Long (for)
35 Disney queen of Arendelle
36 Acorn producer
37 Comrade-in arms
38 Tiny iPods
40 Actor Eric of "Troy" and "Hulk"
41 "Life Is Good" rapper
42 Appropriate anagram for USSR?
43 Headwear for Henri
44 Victorian playhouse associated with Shakespeare
48 Long (for)
49 Workers whose services are on the house?
53 Schedule of meeting items
56 "___ Yankees" (classic Broadway musical)
57 Short snooze
58 Zippo
59 Clay ceramic
62 "The Good Wife" actor Cumming
63 Shortstop's shoe feature
64 Bridle part
65 Tibetan priest
66 Book genre for the DIYer
67 Ringling ___ and Barnum & Bailey

DOWN

1 Nerd's relative
2 Scarlett's surname, in "Gone with the Wind"
3 Type of eel
4 Consume
5 Bar tender?
6 Devoid of ethics
7 "You bet!"
8 Street name in a horror film franchise
9 Tossing and turning
10 Beseech, as a deity
11 Butterfingers' exclamation
12 At the end of the line
13 Creations of Pindar
18 Long-legged marsh wader
23 Costa ___
25 Cockeyed
26 Guthrie whose first album was "Alice's Restaurant"
28 Thick in the head
29 Mighty shout
30 Prince Hamlet, for one
31 Card game that sounds like a command to an annoying feline
32 Yin's counterpart
33 Big name at Ben Gurion Airport
34 "And futhermore ..."
38 Little bird that can climb down tree trunks head first
39 Tennis legend Arthur
40 No-no for a vegetarian
42 Letters on a mailroom stamp
43 Rodeo rider's bucking beast
45 Most-consumed fruit in the United States
46 Turkish peak associated with Noah's ark
47 One-third of a BLT
50 Go into
51 It's sometimes written with a colon
52 Bridges
53 Obsessively neat, in pop psych slang

Utter-ly Familiar

by Elizabeth C. Gorski

Copyright © Devarai GmbH

ACROSS

1 Thanksgiving desserts
5 Roth svgs. plan
8 Scuffles
13 Reserved in manner
15 ___ Moines
16 Also-ran
17 Plane passenger's request
19 Gather
20 Potent stick
21 Personal charm
23 Troubles
24 Serena's sport
28 Milk dispensers?
31 Property claim
33 Tolkien tree creature
34 Yuletide tune
35 Poison ___
36 Sport-___ (rugged vehicle)
37 Procrastinator's motto
41 The Browns, on scoreboards
42 Unruffle one's feathers?
43 Ice cream holder
44 "Have some lasagna!"
45 Stable diet
46 Gave temporarily
48 Least inhibited
50 Holster fillers
51 Isn't any more
54 Lincoln nickname
57 India's first Prime Minister
60 Land in the Irish Sea
62 Virginia Woolf's "___ of One's Own"
63 Erie Canal mule
64 Perpetual traveler
65 Yucky
66 Shed tears
67 Diana of The Supremes

DOWN

1 Exam for a H.S. junior
2 "Don't rub ___!"
3 "___ of Eden"
4 The "S" of RSVP
5 Notions
6 Posterior
7 Sparkling Italian wine
8 Percussive dance of Spain
9 Type of candle or numeral
10 Red ___ beet
11 Thumbs-up
12 H.S. bigwigs
14 Interior design
18 Cows and sows
22 Fulton's power
23 Use a blowtorch
25 Brain cell
26 Sing, as a Gregorian chant
27 Simmered slowly
28 Global relief org. for kids
29 100 cents
30 Erase with a keystroke
31 Troubadours' instruments
32 "___ Fire" (1985 Springsteen hit)
35 Editor's "keep it"
38 Nocturnal marsupials
39 More than mad
40 Some TVs
46 Job for a grease monkey
47 Tie ___ (party hardy)
49 Continental cash
50 "Holy smokes!"
52 Oreo shape
53 Russian ruler
54 Bullets
55 Sheepish replies
56 Concludes
57 Pester
58 Mess up
59 "Yoo-___!"
61 Word on a gift tag

270 degrees

65 Necklace made of leaves and flowers

Repetitive Song Titles

by Patrick Merrell

Copyright © Devarai GmbH

ACROSS

1 Pumpkin-growing plot
6 I.R.S. agent, for short
10 Harm
14 Hawaiian greeting
15 Nevada's "biggest little" gambling city
16 Modern taxi alternative
17 "Sweet" song by The Archies
19 Mechanical learning method
20 Actor Epps or Sharif
21 "Wayne's World" actress Carrere
22 Wizard of Arthurian legend
24 One small sip
27 Gave four stars, for example
28 "Timely" song by The Mamas & the Papas
32 One giving a Bronx cheer
33 Agree, using one's head
34 Rapper ___ Rida
37 Last Supper guest
40 Shellfish, shrimp or shark
43 Nine-digit I.D.
44 Clod
46 "It takes two" dance
47 "Professional" song by Iron Maiden
51 Drew back (from)
54 A "gesundheit" often follows it
55 One-shoed pirate's appendage
57 FedEx competitor
58 Result of paying on credit
62 Meter or inch
63 "Manly" song by The Kingsmen
66 Tantrum throwing star
67 Pitcher in a picture
68 Heartthrob Zac
69 Envisions
70 "Anyone ___ like to try?"
71 Statement when throwing in a poker hand

DOWN

1 El ___, Texas
2 College grad
3 Garment for Caesar
4 "Act it out" party game
5 Laugh syllable
6 Widely accepted statement
7 Huge explosive force
8 Santa ___ Mountains
9 Usual figure
10 "Hip, hip!" follower
11 Letter-shaped fastener
12 Fix loosened shoelaces
13 What's hot, or not
18 Stick around
23 Memorable time period
25 Sour
26 Grandson of Adam
28 Degrees for many CEOs
29 Klutz's word
30 When both hands point straight up
31 President equidistant from FDR and LBJ
34 Family of letters, numbers and other characters
35 Typographic symbol
36 Dumpster emanation, often
38 Position on a map (abbr.)
39 Vittles
41 From ___ (the works)
42 Went up (against)
45 Melted cheese dips
47 River mouths named for their shape
48 Laudatory poem
49 Put back on the payroll
50 Editorial strike out
51 Taters
52 Skating great Sonja
53 Phrase of surrender
56 Musical comedy-drama Fox series
59 Coin of France or Spain
60 Life sci.
61 Work behind a bar
64 Bird that can rotate its head

"Baby, It's Hot!"

by Boris Loring

Copyright © Devarai GmbH

ACROSS

1 Sailed through with flying colors
5 Sudden muscle contraction
10 "Pick a ___ ..."
14 Wild pig
15 Chihuahuan chicken
16 Water that a Chihuahua chicken drinks
17 Troglodyte's dwelling
18 Place to make a sacrifice
19 Decorate, as a Christmas tree
20 Movie segment that may bump the rating from PG 13 to R
23 Density x volume
24 Bobby Fischer's game
25 "Quaking" tree
28 Jim-dandy
31 Hothead's hallmark
34 Shark's foe, in "West Side Story"
37 "Sad to say ..."
38 Furious
39 Pepsi product
40 Decompose
41 Spiky purple wildflower also known as gayfeather
43 Untrue
44 Leader in the electric car market
45 "___ we meet again ..."
48 Coalition
50 Urgent issue to be decided
57 Garfield's canine buddy
58 Circus Maximus, for one
59 "To Live and Die ___" (1985 thriller)
60 A really long time
61 Some domestic workers
62 Chances
63 Examination
64 Middle Crawley daughter on "Downton Abbey"
65 Snack

DOWN

1 Rudimentaries
2 Layer of paint
3 What an icicle might hang from
4 Nickname for undocumented immigrants brought to the United States as youngsters
5 Prevents littering?
6 Voting places
7 Countertenor's counterpart
8 Serb or Croat
9 "Encore!"
10 Like a memorable tune
11 Reach consensus
12 Destroys
13 Judy Dench and Maggie Smith, title wise
21 Lots
22 Harry Potter's forehead feature
25 Somewhere distant
26 Missile site
27 Bog fuel
28 Astound
29 Commercial prefix for "fast" or "plex"
30 Sharp as a tack
32 Cash register's money drawer
33 Cenozoic and Mesozoic, e.g.
34 Notes (down)
35 Airline whose name means "To the Skies" in Hebrew
36 Scarlett O'Hara's plantation
39 Familiar name for a surgical birthing method
41 Indonesian island east of Java
42 Pontiac muscle cars during the 1960s and 1970s
43 Of the best quality
45 WWII German sub
46 Prod gently
47 Attempts
48 Decoratively sculpted baking pan
49 Tether for a terrier
51 Handle
52 Alum
53 Longtime Cunard flagship, briefly
54 ___-European languages
55 Erstwhile GM line, for short
56 Poet Ogden who wrote: "I don't mind eels / Except as meals."

Relatively Speaking

by Kelly Clark

Copyright © Devarai GmbH

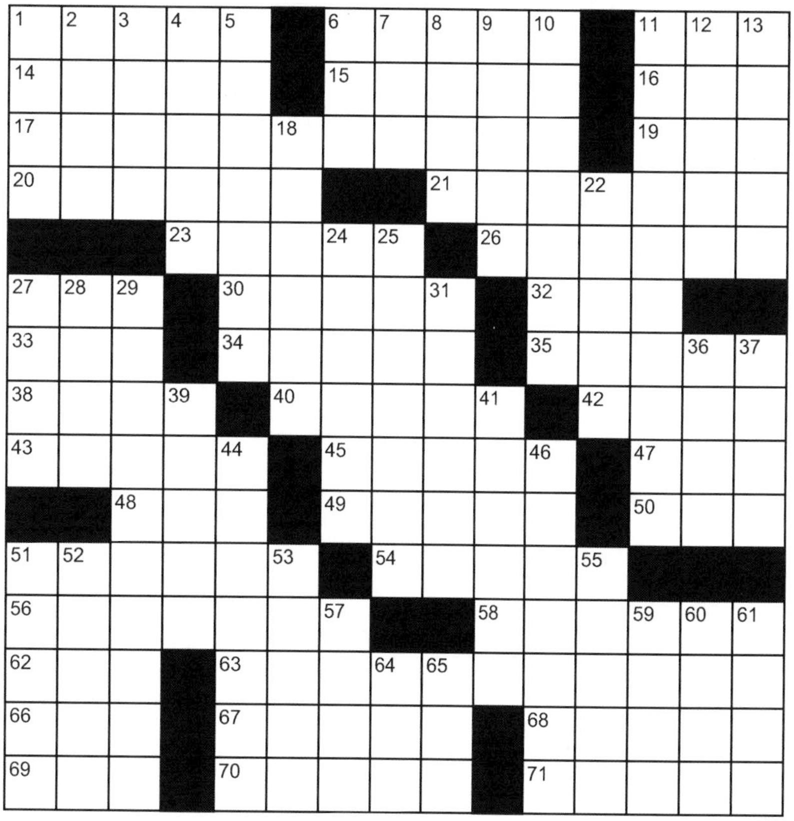

ACROSS

1 Puerto Rico y Cuba
6 Doesn't win
11 No-no for Jack Sprat
14 Redden, as with embarrassment
15 Dadaist Max
16 Grow older
17 Fictitious author of nursery rhymes
19 Scot's topper
20 Globe
21 Marine battler
23 Farm storage structures
26 Sana'a native
27 Pompous sort
30 Bit of thread
32 "___ the land of the free ..."
33 Floral necklace
34 Gal's guy
35 Gown material
38 Sound of astonishment
40 Family members, with "the"
42 Hitchhiker's hope
43 Voices above tenors
45 Absence of musical skill
47 Kitten's cry
48 Building addition shape, often
49 Artful deception
50 Enjoy a meal
51 Skylit courtyard
54 Letter-shaped fastening devices
56 Turns into
58 "Here's to you!" and others
62 Yellowfin tuna
63 2003 Disney comedy-drama
66 Word between "ready" and "go"
67 Church official
68 Former Senator Lott
69 "Listen up!"
70 Enjoys a novel, say
71 Instant decaf brand name

DOWN

1 Many early PCs
2 Feed the hogs
3 Prot. denomination
4 Campfire remains
5 Andy Taylor of Mayberry, for one
6 Table part
7 Spanish gold
8 It's needed for a white Christmas
9 Written homework assignment
10 Sound systems with two or more speakers
11 New Year's Eve icon with a scythe and hourglass
12 Once more
13 Adagio and allegro, e.g.
18 What the Red Cross provides
22 Sling mud at
24 Shaped like a pool table
25 Box office triumph
27 Pond scum
28 Close, as an envelope
29 Another term for "twin town"
31 Earn tons of, as dough
36 Creative spark
37 One-time House Speaker Gingrich
39 Salk vaccine target
41 Military greeting
44 Sleep
46 Sharp comebacks
51 Embarrass
52 Little laugh
53 Haggard of country music
55 Native Israeli
57 Fountain order
59 Witnessed
60 Aquarium, for one
61 Mex. miss
64 Turner of TV channels
65 Store posting: Abbr.

56 Kareem Abdul Jabbar's college alma mater (abbr.)
57 Ran away from
58 "That'll cost an ___ and a leg!"
59 Plaything
60 Biblical figure whose wife was turned into a pillar of salt

Negative Attitudes

by Boris Loring

Copyright © Devarai GmbH

ACROSS

1 Managed to make, with "out"
5 Powder for Junior's butt
9 Swoon
14 Actress Kunis of "Bad Moms"
15 Pitcher Hershiser
16 Islam's highest power
17 "That's my cue!"
18 Prefix for "dynamic" or "nautical"
19 Longhorn cheese, for one
20 Athlete's motto
23 Bakersfield-to Las Vegas dir.
24 6/6/44
25 Salad classically made with anchovies and a raw egg
29 Hip-hop artist born Yasiin Bey
31 Poivre's counterpart, at a French bistro
32 Rawls or Gehrig
33 Natural and uneffected
36 Posse
37 Sex Ed teacher's reminder
41 Makes a midi skirt into a mini
42 Pony up in advance
43 Sought office
44 Sack
46 Sacred songs
50 Faucet
52 Aliens' vehicles, briefly
54 Affirmative in Avignon
55 Cleaning product purveyor's boast
58 Cartographer's compendium
61 Adorable
62 57, in ancient Rome
63 Chicken's perch
64 Scientology founder Hubbard
65 Historical periods
66 Stories about Zeus and Odin
67 Entry in a day calendar (abbr.)
68 Pastrami emporium

DOWN

1 "The Real Slim Shady" rapper
2 Geisha's garb
3 Gets married on the sly
4 "SNL" alumnus Carvey
5 Back, forth, back, forth, ...
6 Madison Square Garden, e.g.
7 Bad bad Brown of song
8 Plumbing woe
9 Spa service
10 Solo
11 Under the weather
12 Snatch
13 "... hallowed be ___ name" (Lord's Prayer phrase)
21 Epitomizing perfection
22 Great card to be dealt in blackjack
26 Czech or Bulgarian
27 Tip-top
28 Toupee, slangily
30 Ph.D.s and B.A.s, for example
31 "Auld Lang ___"
34 Rating for many a sitcom
35 That gal
36 Spanish artist Francisco who shares his name with an Hispanic food brand
37 Opposite of "ebb," tide-wise
38 Prefix for "potent" or "present"
39 Adversary
40 Cowboy's wrangling rope
41 24 of them are in a day (abbr.)
44 Promotes
45 24/7 bank convenience, for short
47 Museum in which "Mona Lisa" resides
48 Baseball's Stan the Man
49 Very emphatic yes, in Barcelona
51 Grind together, as teeth
52 Take by force
53 Photographer's lens setting

or Pearl Jam's Vedder
52 Extreme danger
53 Wipe clean, as a blackboard
54 Summer suit material
55 Filled to the max
56 Therefore
57 Twelve o'clock high
58 Ziggy Stardust's rock genre
59 Comrade-in arms
60 Laze about
61 Inauspicious March day for Caesar
63 H, to Hippocrates

On Fire

by Boris Loring

Copyright © Devarai GmbH

ACROSS

1 Tidy
5 Lobster's meaty appendages
10 Demonstrate
14 "At ___" (military command to relax one's stance)
15 Democratic Republic of the Congo, formerly
16 It's money, according to an aphorism
17 Temporary fixes
20 What those who can't carry a tune are said to have
21 Tutor's tutee
22 Snidely Whiplash's facial expression
23 Very little
24 "One no trump" and "Four hearts," e.g.
27 Piña ___ (tropical cocktail)
32 Bank conveniences that get their highest usage during December (abbr.)
36 Butterfinger's exclamation
38 Superman's name back on Krypton
39 Inconsequential amount
42 Totally exhausted
43 Volvo competitor
44 Big name in corn syrup
45 Doesn't save
47 Luxuriant
49 Actor/rapper who portrays Finn Tutuola on "Law & Order: SVU"
51 German cars with a lightning bolt logo
56 Affianced
60 African country with a capital named for the fifth American president
62 Non-spray way to keep one's pits smelling okay
64 What a soccer player tries to score
65 Information on a book's spine
66 "Got it"
67 "___ honor, I will try ..." (first words of the Girl Scout pledge)
68 Marine critters who can be trained to balance a ball on their nose
69 Give with the expectation of repayment

DOWN

1 Cozy homes
2 Stay home for dinner
3 In a unified fashion
4 Lakota Sioux dwelling
5 Informal designation for the director of the Office of National Drug Control Policy
6 Circuits around the track
7 What you should do before you pull the trigger
8 Gain by force, as control
9 Pacific Northwest airport named for two cities in close proximity
10 Small earring
11 Take on, as an employee
12 Red sky at night, for example
13 Direction of the setting sun
18 Attire
19 Usually 9x9 logic puzzle with numbers
23 Relative of concrete
25 Charged atom
26 They complete lower case i's and j's
28 Insufficiency
29 ___-Seltzer
30 Bambi and his kind
31 Vocal range that means "high"
32 Does sum work
33 Stumble on something
34 Partner of median and mean
35 Gyrate
37 All-Pro linebacker Junior ___
40 The "i" in Roy G. Biv
41 Tiny ammo
46 Olfactory stimuli
48 Tramp
50 Actor Murphy

"Let's Play!"

by Kelly Clark

Copyright © Devarai GmbH

ACROSS

1 "The ___ the limit!"
5 Spill the beans
9 Iron, gold, or silver, e.g.
14 Tech news website
15 Harvard rival
16 Chilling, as champagne: 2 wds.
17 Letter after theta
18 Writer Hunter
19 "SNL" airer
20 Benny Goodman played during this period: 3 wds.
23 24-hour period
24 Generic, as a brand: 2 wds.
28 Eastman-Kodak's "Carousel-S," for one: 2 wds.
33 Jazz guy Getz and baseball's Musial
34 Angels' head toppers, in art
35 Harem room
36 Makes a boo boo
37 "Sweetheart"
38 Chemical suffixes
39 So-so grade
40 "In God We Trust" for the United States, e.g.
41 Degrade
42 U.S. president for whom a toy bear is named after: 2 wds.
45 "Saturday Night Live" skits, e.g.
46 "What's the ___?" ("What does it matter?" in slang)
47 Musical featuring the character "Nathan Detroit": 3 wds.
54 Like testimony made under oath
57 Jai ___
58 Source
59 Any "Friends" episode, today
60 Seward Peninsula city
61 Beige
62 Expressionless, as a poker-face
63 Beholds
64 Barely managed, with "out"

DOWN

1 Chem. and bio., e.g.
2 Be certain
3 Abominable Snowman
4 Substitutes: hyph.
5 "Ta-ta!": hyph.
6 Volcano flow
7 Alda of "M*A*S*H"
8 Road curve
9 President James and actress Marilyn
10 With all judges present: 2 wds.
11 ___-tac-toe
12 Make a move
13 Bk. after Exodus
21 Gallivants, with "about"
22 Take pleasure in
25 Without a key, musically
26 Unlike a braggart
27 Wipe the slate clean
28 Actress Meryl who played Thatcher
29 Texas city on the Rio Grande
30 Snapshot
31 Totaled, as a cost: 2 wds.
32 Fake butter bread spreads
33 Religious splinter groups
37 Merry-go round figure, to a tot
38 "___, except after C...": 3 wds. (and there are SO many exceptions to this spelling rule!)
40 "___ Valentine" (jazz standard): 2 wds.
41 All fired up
43 Area to exercise a kennel resident: 2 wds.
44 Whirlpools
48 Without: Fr.
49 Medicinal plant
50 "Kelly," e.g.
51 Diary fastener
52 Tales handed down
53 Type of earring
54 12th graders: Abbr.
55 Rainy
56 Spanish gold

Eat Dessert First!

by Elizabeth C. Gorski

Copyright © Devarai GmbH

ACROSS

1 Maple tree product
4 Brought back to health
9 Sharp tooth
13 School support org.
14 Atmospheric layer
15 Old photo tint
16 Unit of corn
17 Empty promise
19 Cover story?
21 Entryway
22 Wide shoe width
23 Outcomes
26 General ___ chicken (Chinese entrée)
28 Identical
33 Prohibit
36 Buffoon
37 Is gaga over
38 Trendy antioxidant berry
40 Recipe abbr.
42 Poet Whitman
43 "The Bathers" painter
46 ___ Major
49 Sch. in East Lansing
50 Credit for good behavior
53 Electrical letters
54 Takes a nap
58 Yellow vehicle
61 "The ___ Duckling"
63 Motionless
64 John Brim song covered by Van Halen
68 Member of a sting operation?
69 Some are whitewalls
70 Words of defeat
71 "Red Seal" record co.
72 Rim
73 "When it ___, it pours"
74 The Braves, on scoreboards

DOWN

1 Asparagus unit
2 Dickens title starter
3 Eiffel Tower locale
4 Member of a flight crew
5 Submachine gun
6 Sturgeon product
7 Oklahoma city
8 Signify
9 Service charge
10 Church area
11 Goddess of victory
12 "Mercy Mercy Me" singer Marvin
15 Sacred treasure of Turin
18 Puccini opera
20 Tampa Bay player, briefly
24 AAA job
25 "SNL" segment
27 Pack cargo
29 "___ to you" ("Your call")
30 Disneyland shuttle
31 Snakelike swimmers
32 Queue after Q
33 Biting remark
34 Maker of Aspire PCs
35 Small iPod
39 The Hawkeye State
41 Experts
44 Racks up, as debt
45 Corduroy feature
47 Fall from grace
48 Blesses with oil
51 Cream-filled pastry
52 2,000 pounds
55 Striped equine
56 Build, as a skyscraper
57 Take something the wrong way?
58 Refer to
59 Car battery fluid
60 Floating ice mass
62 Classic Village People song
65 So-so grade
66 ___ tai (tiki bar cocktail)
67 Raggedy doll

Setting the Stage

by Elizabeth C. Gorski

Copyright © Devarai GmbH

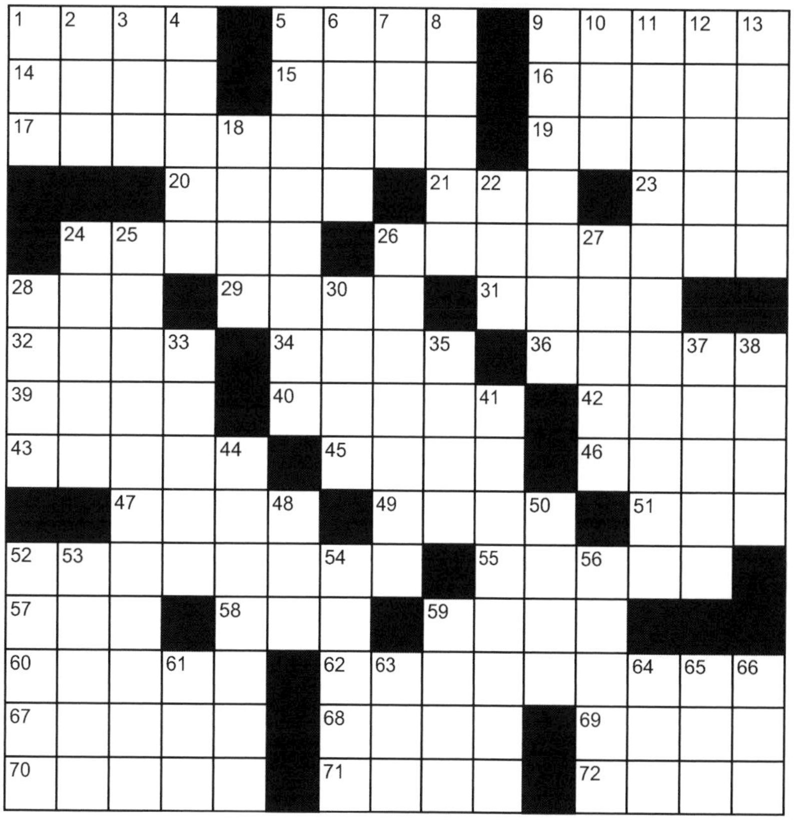

ACROSS

1 Proper partner?
5 Boston ___ Orchestra
9 Joy of "The View"
14 Conceal
15 From square one
16 Off to ___ start (delayed)
17 Raffle reward, perhaps
19 Arm bones
20 Trevi Fountain toss-in
21 Sports fig.
23 AMA members
24 Out of whack
26 Gooey slapstick missile
28 "Game of Thrones" channel
29 Biblical pronoun
31 Hawaiian feast
32 Takes a course?
34 Rival of Glamour and Allure
36 March 17 parade honoree, for short
39 Tennis legend Arthur
40 Epsom ___
42 Duel tool
43 Scarlett's suitor
45 "Taken" star Neeson
46 Crime lab fluids
47 Regrets
49 Czech or Pole, e.g.
51 Heisman winner Tebow
52 Baba ganoush ingredient
55 Put an end to
57 Earth (Pref.)
58 Brit's restroom
59 Gumbo veggie
60 Parts of molecules
62 Like some designer apparel
67 '70's dance spot, for short
68 More than
69 Word of approval
70 Oktoberfest vessel
71 Without
72 Scruff

DOWN

1 Prof's degree
2 Carnival city
3 Altar affirmative
4 "Thank you, Henri"
5 Diocese subdivisions
6 Getting ___ years
7 Dispensable candy brand
8 Use cuss-words
9 German art school of the 1920s
10 Right angle
11 Kukla and Ollie, but not Fran
12 Computer game pioneer
13 Witherspoon of "Legally Blonde"
18 Military assignment
22 ___ Aviv University
24 Shame
25 "Maternal" nursery rhyme author
26 String quartet player
27 Australian "buddies"
28 Learn (of)
30 Mideast airline
33 Arrangement
35 And others (Lat.)
37 High nest
38 Athletic squad
41 Dollars, informally
44 Rats out, kid style
48 ___ Paulo, Brazil
50 Part of speech
52 Quaint exclamation
53 Jokester's question
54 Taboos
56 Packers quarterback ___ Rodgers
59 Mystical sign
61 1101, Roman style
63 Glamorous Gardner
64 Alias letters
65 Snooze
66 Decorate Easter eggs

T.G.I.F.!

by Elizabeth C. Gorski

Copyright © Devarai GmbH

ACROSS

1 Basil and rosemary, e.g.
6 Venetian blind part
10 Jet speed measure
14 James and Tommie
15 Birthplace of Galileo
16 Jacob's brother
17 1997 Robin Williams film
20 Bygone Brit. Airways jet
21 Evil anagram/synonym
22 Hopping mad
23 Tehran resident
25 Roman 1051
26 Quarterback with four Super Bowl rings
30 Bean ___ (tofu)
34 Mountains of Peru
35 Standard
37 "Norma ___"
38 Sweet dinner course
41 Dried grapes
43 Summer in Paris
44 Poet Teasdale
46 "You can ___ horse ..."
47 Hand (out)
49 Stylish-and-relaxed fashion sense
52 Scot's refusal
54 Pie-in-the face sound
55 Radiant glows
58 Puff piece?
59 "I think, therefore ___"
62 Hit single on Santana's "Abraxas" album
66 Military group
67 "___ It Romantic?"
68 Opening, for short
69 Shades of summer
70 Snooping around
71 Road curves

DOWN

1 Storybook witch
2 Swelled heads
3 Classic autos
4 When kids are tucked in
5 Away from NNE
6 Limb immobilizer
7 Playwright Hellman
8 Wimbledon singles winner of 1975
9 Greek cross
10 Like liters and grams
11 China setting?
12 Quitter's word
13 Ginormous
18 "Terrible" tsar
19 Zero
24 Valentine's Day bouquet
25 Kate of "The Martian"
26 World-weary
27 "___ a customer, please"
28 Son of Henry Ford
29 Fish-fowl insert
31 Heep who's a creep
32 "Amazing" illusionist
33 Cul-___ (dead end street)
36 Actress Jovovich
39 Indy event
40 ___-la-la
42 Newspaper divisions
45 Gives, as homework
48 Passes (a law)
50 Putting on airs
51 Sir Guinness
53 Pop the question
55 Border on
56 Forearm bone
57 April forecast
58 El ___, Texas
60 Small quantities?
61 Stable mom
63 Hr. fraction
64 Golfer Michelle
65 Refusals

Let It Snow, Let It Snow, Let It Snow

by Patrick Merrell

Copyright © Devarai GmbH

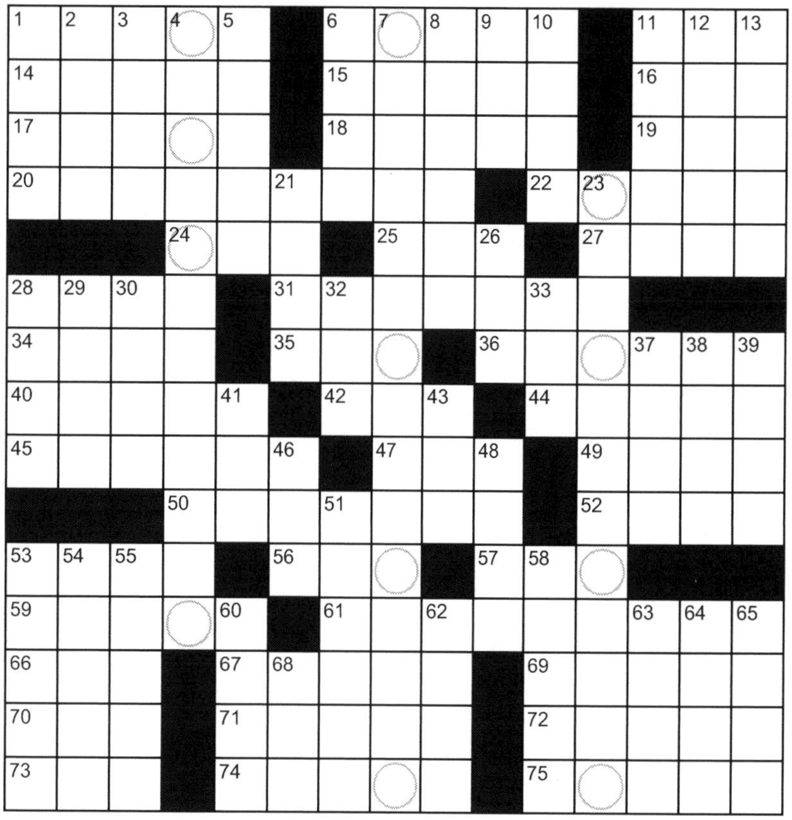

ACROSS

1 What ignorance is, in a phrase
6 Holy hymn
11 No. 2's
14 Add lanes to, as a highway
15 Courtroom figs.
16 Anger
17 Essential ___ acids
18 Less common
19 Picky little complaint
20 Baseball player who said "The future ain't what it used to be"
22 Univ. course for aspiring therapists
24 East, in Essen
25 "___ the season to be jolly ..."
27 Soccer chants
28 Off in the distance
31 "Could that be?"
34 Use a board, at the beach
35 Seemingly endless wait
36 U.S. resident, slangily
40 Practiced, as a trade
42 Ones turned in a book (abbr.)
44 Supposed baby deliverer
45 Ski event with gates
47 From ___ z (the gamut)
49 Double-reeded instrument
50 Fills, as a moving van
52 Come clean, with "up"
53 Run of the mill
56 Corp. head
57 Words of commitment
59 Divided down the middle
61 What awaits the dead, in many beliefs
66 Goat's cry
67 X-rated stuff
69 More mature
70 Inexpensive pen brand
71 Threesomes
72 Striped barber shop signs
73 The most famous one was made of gopher wood
74 Meat-and potatoes potfuls
75 Stockholm native

DOWN

1 NYC street lit with lots of neon
2 V.I.P.'s vehicle
3 "Groovy, man"
4 High-ranking member of a think tank
5 Hoity-toity types
6 Catherine ___, Henry VIII's last wife
7 From this moment on
8 Transport in a Duke Ellington song
9 Cleaning solution
10 Inits. on a new car sticker
11 LP record material
12 Number on a store tag
13 MacFarlane and Rogen
21 Suffix meaning "small"
23 Coming shortly
26 What's up?
28 They're "unarmed," but dangerous
29 Stuffed to the gills
30 Operatic solo
32 Make like a kangaroo
33 KLM competitor
37 Expensive steak variety from Japan
38 Arrow-shooting god
39 Barely makes, with "out"
41 Scooby-___
43 Man's name whose letters are alphabetically consecutive
46 PC alternative
48 Mayberry boy
51 Hon
53 Mufasa's boy in "The Lion King"
54 Sign at a radio station
55 Pancake order
58 Plummets
60 Makes a pick
62 Fling
63 Not working
64 Give a meal to
65 Celtic tongue
68 Leftover

47 Short socks
49 Like bony knees
50 Cash register key used to open the drawer without a transaction
51 Womb
52 Inventor known as the Wizard of Menlo Park
53 Site of a famous "When Harry Met Sally ..." scene
54 It goes "Pop!" in a children's song
59 Spittoon user's sound
61 Fabricated
62 Green Gables gal
63 Neb.'s northern neighbor
65 "Incidentally," to a texter
66 Caviar
67 Q-U connection

Shifting Sand

by Boris Loring

Copyright © Devarai GmbH

ACROSS

1 Injure
5 Part of speech that shows tense
9 Wispy clusters ... or a Massachusetts university
14 Southern California city that sounds like a surprised greeting
15 Furniture chain based in Sweden
16 Culotte kin
17 Junior Seau, for the first 13 years of his career
20 Blackmail
21 UPC-like product ID
22 ___ pickle (facing trouble)
23 Ice hockey player's milieu
25 Examine closely
28 Fictional Pottsylvanian spies who answered to Fearless Leader on "The Bullwinkle Show"
32 Purchase
33 Erstwhile Soviet space station
34 Convent resident
35 Fundamental set of beliefs
38 Oolong or jasmine
40 "Cool!"
44 Ltd.'s American cousin
46 Jamaican music genre
48 Female sib
49 Fist in the face, in quaint slang
55 Reporter's writing tablet
56 __-Ball (carnival game)
57 Suffix for many simple sugars
58 Tear
60 Beasts of burden in the Andes
64 Actress/singer who won an Oscar for her role in "Funny Girl"
68 Belushi's "Animal House" character, familiarly
69 Evict from office
70 Given name of artist St. Vincent Millay
71 "___ Can!" (Obama campaign slogan)
72 Cooties
73 Scallion-like vegetable in a classic vichyssoise

DOWN

1 Fireman's hydrant attachment
2 Household cleanser that shares a name with a Greek warrior
3 Harangue
4 Sweet melon flavored green liqueur ... or the first name of Japanese figureskating great Ito
5 "Platoon" setting
6 Ticker tape?
7 Speed Wagons and Flying Clouds
8 Use the "Reverse" gear to park
9 Suitcase searching airport gp.
10 Kiev's country (abbr.)
11 Fuddy-duddies
12 Ditch
13 Layers of rock ... or a savory dish similar to a bread pudding
18 Colored part of the eye
19 Chinese province known for its crispy orange beef
24 Create a cardigan sweater, maybe
26 Astound
27 Sheet of glass
28 U.K. media letters
29 Your + my
30 Pumpernickel alternative
31 Add Ranch to the salad
36 Cubes rolled in a game of craps
37 Like a G.I. peeling potatoes
39 Aliases, for short
41 "___ live and breathe!"
42 Partner of tac and toe
43 ___Kosh B'Gosh (kids' clothing company)
45 Pioneering nurse Barton

"But I Repeat Myself"

by Kelly Clark

Copyright © Devarai GmbH

ACROSS

1 "The King and I" setting
5 Wealthy
9 Sulk
13 Prefix with dextrous
14 Crucifix letters
15 Crept furtively
16 *Nude, nude: 2 wds,
18 "Jack Sprat could ___ fat...": 2 wds.
19 Master, in Swahili
20 Ocean front
22 "That feels good!"
23 *Before, before: 2 wds.
27 "___-la-la" (sung syllable)
28 Prefix with puncture
29 "Do it my way, ___ quit!":2 wds.
30 December 24 or 31
31 Skirt lines
33 Land in l'océan
35 Beginning
37 What the answer-phrases to the starred clues are
41 Board, as a train: 2 wds.
44 A billion years
45 Hefner of "Playboy Magazine"
49 She played Lisa in "Green Acres"
50 Clampett of 1960s TV
53 Demolition stuff: Abbr.
55 Scot's denial
56 *Blend, blend: 2 wds.
59 Israeli weapon
60 Colorful brand name?
61 Simplifies
63 Like day-old bread, sometimes
64 *Outcome, outcome: 2 wds.
67 Doled (out)
68 "Yay! The work-week is almost over!" Abbr.
69 Wan
70 Fruity coolers
71 Looked over
72 Winter downhill vehicle

DOWN

1 Day of rest, especially in Judaism
2 "This is not news to me": 2 wds.
3 President Lincoln
4 Demeanor
5 River inlet
6 Calligrapher's purchase
7 Colgate rival
8 Cab Calloway's signature line :hyph.
9 Braid of hair
10 Is more successful than
11 Discombobulate
12 Boxing ref's ring decision: Abbr.
15 Meeting
17 California wine valley
21 Tire filler
24 Etcher's need
25 "Star Trek" helmsman
26 "You ain't seen nothin' ___!"
32 "No seats left" sign letters
34 U-turn from WSW
36 To the ___ degree
38 Took pleasure in
39 "The lady ___ protest too much": Shakespeare
40 "Green Gables" girl
41 Precious stone
42 Bounced out by the landlord
43 Internal Revenue Service ratio: 2 wds.
46 Odd
47 Graceful small antelope
48 Committed robbery
51 Freudian topic
52 Erase, on a computer
54 Joyce Kilmer subject, in a poem
57 Stories
58 Sharp-tasting
62 Egyptian snakes
63 Wee, to Burns
65 Conk out, as an engine
66 U.S.P.S. countryside system, once: Abbr.

54 Dr. Franken-stein's lab assistant
55 Fine cotton
56 Jet black, or a stone of that color
59 Tiny bit
60 Ghost's shout

"House of Cards"

by Boris Loring

Copyright © Devarai GmbH

ACROSS

1 Sweet-scented purple flower
6 Hole-making tools
10 Pequod commander
14 Type of acid that's an essential building block of protein
15 Tree's "foot"
16 Lady who calls her fans "little monsters"
17 Conflict ended with the Paris Peace Accords
19 Not odd
20 Archconservative Coulter
21 First year of the 3rd century, to Diocletian
22 Insanity
24 Garners
26 Up to now
27 Bellagio or the Venetian, for example
33 Sun Devils' Arizona home
34 Fruit that gives it name to the German word for lightbulb
35 Scooby-___
36 Thor's dad
37 John Bates's Downton Abbey position
39 Oodles
40 Eldest of Louisa May Alcott's "little women"
41 ___-pedi
42 William and Harry's mum
43 Iconic Big Apple landmark completed in 1883
47 A/C capacity meas.
48 Hula skirt material
49 Ingredient in many a salad dressing
53 Not forward
54 Privately held company's "coming out" event (abbr.)
57 Online auction giant
58 Homemade booze
61 Sing praises
62 Actor Neeson
63 Spacious
64 Produced offspring
65 Odds' partners
66 Household cleaner that used to be advertised with a 20-mule team

DOWN

1 Ooze emanating from Iceland's Eyjafjallajökul
2 Declaration of a confident poker player
3 Security interest, such as a mortgage
4 Pesky picnic spoiler
5 Curved inward
6 Providing weapons to
7 Amazed interjection
8 Fertile soil
9 Homeless feline
10 Jerry Maguire and his colleagues, by profession
11 Possess
12 A very long time
13 Forbids
18 1/640 of a square mile
23 Start of a letter's salutation
24 Jocks' channel
25 Baby tree
27 Hosen material
28 Puebla pal
29 Visualize
30 It may be found on Fido's collar
31 Nary a soul
32 Actress Chaplin of "Game of Thrones"
33 Mausoleum's contents
37 Worth a pretty penny
38 "___ Given Sunday" (Pacino movie)
39 Helps out
41 Business school subj.
42 Unsettle
44 Heeded
45 19th century composer of a famed lullaby
46 Huckleberry Finn's transportation down the Mississippi River
49 Hit or miss?
50 Construction worker's need
51 Cathedral section that sounds like a deceitful fellow
52 April precipitation

tion

"It's Tea Time!"

by Kelly Clark

Copyright © Devarai GmbH

ACROSS

1 Like Midwestern accents (to non-Midwesterners)
6 Cardinal ___ O'Malley, Archbishop of Boston
10 Pageant contestant's wear
14 Muscat native
15 Cookbook author Rombauer
16 It's a thought
17 Ship's sail supporters
18 Happy
19 Negative votes in Paris
20 Win big-time: 3 wds.
23 Vegetable in a pod
25 Have a bite
26 Like something so out...it's back in!
27 Science fiction vehicles: 2 wds.
32 Truck drivers who are often "good buddies," in brief
33 Got bigger
34 "Smooth Operator" singer
35 Size below medium
37 ___- sci (college class in gov't)
41 Feathery scarves
42 Sudden, uncontrollable fear
43 Hillbilly couple who first appeared in the movie "The Egg and I": 4 wds.
47 Happen
49 Adult boy
50 "___ a boy!" (contraction)
51 National Hockey League trophy: 3 wds.
56 Hauls, as a broken down car
57 "Crazy" bird
58 The "I" in I.V.
61 "La Bamba" actor Morales
62 Affectionate, like some farewells
63 Detroit football team
64 Artist Magritte
65 "Iliad" warrior
66 The turf in "surf and turf"

DOWN

1 ___ de plume (pen name)
2 Physicians' org.
3 Walked ostentatiously
4 Pro's opposite
5 Pays attention (to)
6 What a tourist sees, with "the"
7 Author ___ Stanley Gardner
8 Key of Beethoven's Seventh: Abbr.
9 "Nothing," in Spain
10 "Hook, line, and ___"
11 Takes in, as a homeless child
12 Madrid Mister
13 Must: 2 wds.
21 "You're it" kid's game
22 Ship's personnel
23 In the Army, they're ranked below corporals: Abbr.
24 Napoleon's isle of exile
28 Extreme rage
29 Showing shock
30 Website address: Abbr.
31 Disney collectible
35 Second Person of the Trinity, with "the"
36 Like the hatter in "Alice in Wonderland"
37 Bit of butter
38 Walking very quietly, say: 2 wds.
39 Cheery tune
40 Frosts, as a cake
41 Homer Simpson's boy
42 Lead-filled writing instruments
43 Ian who wrote "Atonement"
44 Sydney resident, informally
45 Makes right
46 Mary ___ Cosmetics
47 Aquatic mammal
48 Selected
52 ___ Romeo (Italian auto)
53 Koh-i-___ diamond
54 "The ___ Ranger"
55 Condo, e.g.
59 Genetic info carrier
60 Pop the ques-

Jurassic creature
55 Professor 'Iggins in "My Fair Lady"
57 Credit alternative at the checkout counter
58 Where the femur meets the tibia
59 Tree of Life garden
60 Cookbook amts.
62 Plus
63 Mag.'s output

The U.S. of 4 A's

by Patrick Merrell

Copyright © Devarai GmbH

ACROSS

1 Tight football players?
5 Not appropriate
10 Wee woolly one
14 Rent-___ (night watchman)
15 Aristocratic
16 Melting stick in a crafter's gun
17 Geological feature that might cause "the big one" in California
20 Body art
21 Suffix with electro-
22 Roast hosts, for short
23 Unruly group
25 Like an outfit covered in sequins or glitter
27 Popular tourist attraction between Lake Ontario and Lake Erie
33 Upright
34 Service branch with aircraft carriers
35 Send via FedEx
39 "Dumb ___ so dumb ..."
40 One ___ time
41 Kitchen strainer
42 Wintertime precipitation
43 Medical or figure drawing subj.
44 Channel with Capitol Hill coverage
45 Mountains that extend from Alabama to Canada
48 Matching while marching
51 Outback hopper
52 Co.'s head honcho
53 Medicine amount
56 One launched from Cape Canaveral
61 Group that includes Oahu
64 Rates ___ (is perfect)
65 Operating room assistant
66 Ooze
67 Chuck of "Meet the Press"
68 Lovers' rendezvous
69 Barnyard brooders

DOWN

1 To the right, on a map
2 March Madness org.
3 "Cut it out!"
4 Smallish quarrel
5 Word before pool, plumbing or plant
6 "... ___ gloom of night stays these couriers ..."
7 Cain's brother
8 Theater production
9 Try out a new plane
10 Airport alternative to JFK
11 College reunion attendees, briefly
12 Garden soil covering
13 Flag-making Ross
18 People with an on-the move lifestyle
19 Dropped
24 Fruit with a peel
26 St. Francis's birthplace
27 Makes a silent bid
28 Aware of, as a plan
29 Prefix with space at a Smithsonian museum
30 Chew on, as a beaver might
31 Deadly
32 2009 blockbuster featuring blue skinned Pandorans
36 Type of air filter in some vacuums
37 "Terrible" Russian leader
38 Handouts after some presidential signings
41 Building with lockers and a lunchroom
43 Name, to an office
46 Mani's partner, in nail salon slang
47 Waist-pinching wear
48 Onetime Apple messaging tool
49 "Peachy!"
50 Planted, as wild oats
54 Name ender for many a

"To Coin Some Phrases..."

by Kelly Clark

Copyright © Devarai GmbH

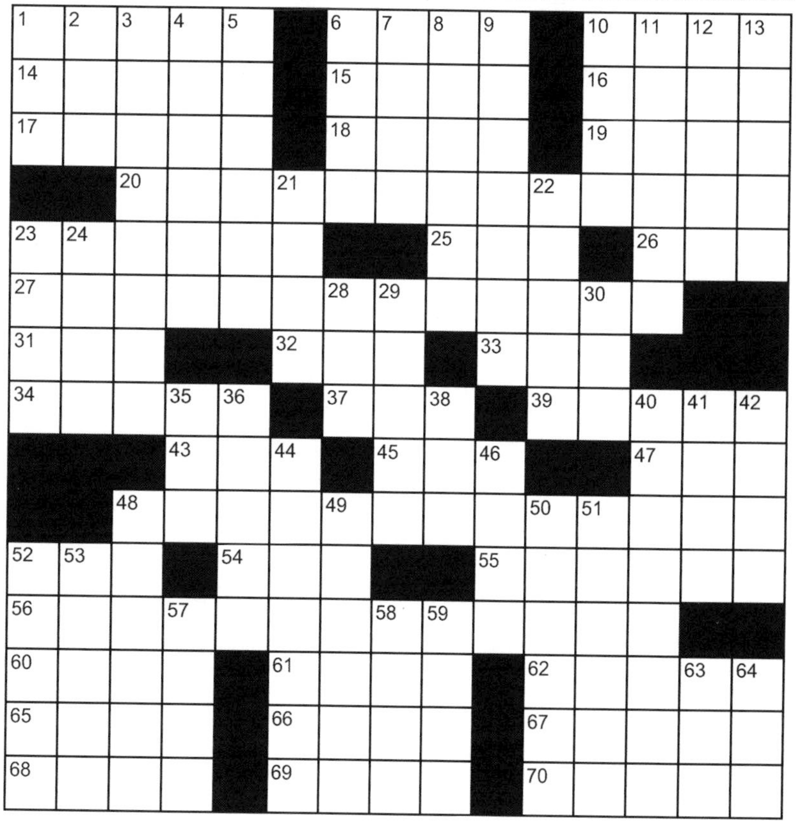

ACROSS

1 California missionary Junipero ___
6 Important restaurant employee
10 Luau strings
14 Welcome
15 Sagan of "Cosmos"
16 Metered vehicle
17 "Jerusalem Delivered" poet Torquato
18 Actor Robert De___
19 Like the Sahara
20 She played Laverne on "Laverne & Shirley"
23 Where Athens is
25 Tiny criticism
26 Golf ball prop
27 Of little importance
31 Quantity: Abbr.
32 Heavy-duty cleanser
33 Apple pie ___ mode
34 Boxer Mike
37 Musician's asset
39 Pepe ___ (amorous cartoon skunk)
43 No good
45 Olympian's dream score
47 "Uncle Tom's Cabin" girl
48 "Be merciless!"
52 Bank loan letters
54 "Who am ___ judge?"
55 Like gala attire
56 A move to a different attitude
60 Crime scene barrier
61 Peevish state
62 Makes cat calls?
65 Employs
66 President William Howard ___
67 How Santa Claus dresses, for the most part
68 Annoying one
69 Barbershop sound
70 Editorial deletion undoers

DOWN

1 Cpl.'s superior
2 Important time period
3 Thinks highly of
4 Look for again
5 "Right now!"
6 Big Apple sch.
7 Onetime teen idol Corey
8 Item on a "to do" list
9 Miami's state
10 Great Salt Lake's state
11 Discipline with chops and kicks
12 Napoleon on Elba, e.g.
13 Move like a crab
21 Dudley Do Right's love
22 Motionless
23 Itsy-bitsy biter
24 Frost-covered
28 Sailor's affirmative
29 "Peachy!"
30 West of "My Little Chickadee"
35 Geisha's sash
36 Ship's course plotting: Abbr.
38 Mandatory coll. course
40 Place to buy a goldfish
41 Nights before
42 Cautious
44 Absolutely can't stand
46 Without a stitch on
48 Wine-making needs
49 Wall Street Journal columnist Peggy
50 One of the Three Musketeers
51 Sublet an apartment, say
52 Misbehave
53 New moon, e.g.
57 Hatchling's home
58 Stereotypical name for a French poodle
59 URL starter
63 Soaked
64 1960s college political org.

World Shopping Spree

by Elizabeth C. Gorski

Copyright © Devarai GmbH

ACROSS

1 Earth Day subj.
5 Shredded cabbage salad
9 "Shoo!"
13 Willy of "Death of a Salesman"
15 Feeling achy
16 Marco, the world traveler
17 Crunchy snacks purchased in Rio?
19 Miles away
20 Infuriate
21 Pig's pen
23 Shark's appendage
24 Lasso
27 Horse's father
29 Thanksgiving meals purchased in Istanbul?
33 "The Godfather" enforcer Luca
35 Oboe insert
36 Minor quarrel
37 Losing tic-tac toe line
38 "Honest" president
40 Neighbor of Syr.
42 Eggs, in labs
43 Roman 1601
45 "Quickly!" in a memo
47 Daisylike fall flower
49 Warm-weather attire purchased at a resort?
52 This, to Julio
53 Job offerer
54 Auction action
56 Software program, briefly
58 Praises mightily
62 "Nurse Jackie" star Falco
64 Hot-weather toppers purchased in a canal zone?
67 David Bowie's "___ Dance"
68 Told a fib
69 Stately home
70 Opposite of first
71 Finishes
72 Snoozing breaks

DOWN

1 Hamburg's river
2 Veggie on a cob
3 Sharif of "Funny Girl"
4 New Testament miracle recipient
5 Payroll ID number
6 Singer Rawls
7 The "A" of NEA
8 "___ Story" (Broadway musical with the hit song "Maria")
9 Rejuvenating resort
10 Brewing vessels at a breakfast meeting
11 Jai ___
12 Ripped up
14 Most populous African country
18 Drippy faucet problem
22 Yang's partner
25 Mother ___ (Nobel Peace Prize winner)
26 Senate assent
28 Hosp. staffers
29 Reductions on an IRS form
30 Famous oracle locale
31 5-star film review
32 Christmas tree topper
33 Box office flop
34 Traveled by horse
39 No-goodnik
41 Law grad's hurdle
44 Quick AOL exchanges
46 Volcano fallout
48 Former NFL star Michael who's a co-anchor on "Good Morning America"
50 Stage actress Hagen
51 Utah city
54 Noisy neck accessory for a cow
55 Brainstorm
57 Aspirin's target
59 Turner of Hollywood
60 Sporty automobile roof
61 Cold War countries (Abbr.)
63 Superlative suffix
65 Beatty or Rorem
66 TV commercials

the suburbs
52 Playful river or sea mammal
53 People online
54 Lindsay of "Freaky Friday"
55 Salad garnish that can also have "water" as a prefix
58 Disney's "___ and the Detectives"
59 Easy sports victory
60 Rogers and Orbison
63 Cheer during a toro's charge
64 Org. that screens airplane passengers
65 Valuable mining find

Knock Knock Jokes

by Patrick Merrell

Copyright © Devarai GmbH

ACROSS

1 There are five on the back wheel of a 10 speed bike
6 Men whose names sound like they're cars
11 Dashboard navigation aid, for short
14 Mumbai's country
15 Hang out in a henhouse
16 Started, as a bonfire
17 Knock knock. Who's there? Etch. Etch who?
19 Q-tip target
20 Donkey
21 Without ___ (free of charge)
22 Singer Summer or designer Karan
24 Knock knock. Who's there? Guess. Guess who?
27 Liquid part of blood
30 Super Bowl LII sportscaster Collinsworth
31 Pause in the conversation
32 Type of list that's often counted down
35 "That's ___ an option"
38 Carrying weapons
40 Knock knock. Who's there? Spell. Spell who?
41 Travelocity's cone-hatted mascot
43 reply
44 Giving the once over, visually
47 Terrible Russian tsar
48 Mosque leader
49 Academy Awards
51 Knock knock. Who's there? Tank. Tank who?
56 On a ship in the ocean
57 Popular Nabisco cookie
58 Make mistakes
61 Numbered roadway (abbr.)
62 Knock knock. Who's there? Cows go. Cows go who?
66 ___ Spiegel (German magazine)
67 "___ Dream" ("Lohengrin" aria)
68 Covered with grit and dirt
69 H.S. graduating class
70 University officials
71 Shrill barks

DOWN

1 Prefix with byte or hertz
2 Grandson of Adam
3 Does some basic math
4 Chest bone
5 Peaceful Middle East greeting
6 Canadian skating great Brian
7 "Move along, folks! Nothing ___ here!"
8 Item made in Santa's workshop
9 Bear, in Spanish
10 Preparing for a test
11 Actress Close
12 Musical instrument with keys, pedals, and a bench
13 Building material for the first little pig
18 D-sharp equivalent
23 Approves, briefly
24 Spot of land in the ocean
25 Follow, as advice
26 Dr. of rap
27 School recess activity
28 Fishing decoy
29 Payment to the poor
33 "I'll get the money from you later"
34 ___ Beta Kappa
35 Exploding star
36 Poet Khayyam
37 Yellow Monopoly bills
39 Humiliated
42 Pleasant
45 Rotate, as a rocket
46 Like hot fudge or roasted marshmallows
48 Anger
50 Like the air in Beijing or Los Angeles, often
51 Front and back areas, in

Seize the Day!

by Elizabeth C. Gorski

Copyright © Devarai GmbH

ACROSS

1 Earnest appeal
5 Washington D.C.'s Capitol ___
9 Wise people
14 Skipper's place
15 Berry in a healthy smoothie
16 Politico and industrialist ___ Perot
17 Simplicity
18 Baseball team
19 Playful river critter
20 Leo Sayer hit song covered by Rod Stewart
23 Driving need?
24 More ventilated
28 Traffic sign at an intersection
32 Suspicious
34 Victories
35 Frenzied
36 ___ Romeo (Italian car)
37 Out of whack
39 Do a critic's job
40 Roman 1002
41 Military division
42 Prevent, as crime
43 Lena Horne song composed by Harold Arlen
47 Biblical dancer
48 Nanki-___ ("The Mikado" role)
49 On several occasions
56 Safari heavyweight
59 Silly mistake
60 Disapproving shouts
61 Film trophy
62 Vampire novelist Rice
63 Swelled heads
64 Solemn promises
65 Antelope's playmate
66 Contemporary "carpe diem" that's spelled out at the ends of 20-, 28-, 43- and 49-Across

DOWN

1 "Man, that was close!"
2 Wife of Jacob
3 Otherwise
4 "So be it"
5 "Splash" star Daryl
6 Least friendly
7 Bowling spot
8 Made up a story
9 Sure winners
10 Maestro Toscanini
11 "You've ___ Mail"
12 Compass pt.
13 Estonia, once (Abbr.)
21 Punk-rocker ___ Pop
22 Tales of the sea
25 Pen pal?
26 Fill with joy
27 ___ Cup (golf trophy)
28 Second cup of coffee
29 Lyricist Gershwin
30 Buffoons
31 Sue Grafton's "___ for Undertow"
32 Tibetan priests
33 "Clueless" actress Donovan
37 Rage
38 "Mamma ___" (ABBA song)
39 Gun the engine
41 Detaches from a dock
42 Pop singer Céline
44 Tuba sound
45 Apple Store purchase
46 Slip-on shoe
50 "Zounds!"
51 Vocal quality
52 Follow orders
53 NASA cancellation
54 Refrigerate
55 Canadian gas brand
56 "Yoo-___!"
57 Patience ___ virtue
58 Agt.'s cut

32 Create, as havoc
36 Pertaining to the area around the South Pole
37 Principal
38 Drove faster than 55 mph, perhaps
40 Viral phenomenon on the internet
42 Working stiff's exclamation of relief
45 Middle East emirate
47 Custom-made products
50 Cash register key used to open the drawer without a transaction
51 It disappears when you stand up
52 CNN medical expert Sanjay
53 Plant ___ of doubt
54 Swashbuckler played on the silver screen by Antonio Banderas
58 Blood type of approximately 1.5% of the American population, briefly
59 Thickening agent
60 Make a fool of
62 Wee bit, or the ninth letter of the Greek alphabet
63 Exam
65 Bro's female sib
66 Auction unit

"Pussies Galore"

by Boris Loring

Copyright © Devarai GmbH

ACROSS

1 Take a load off one's feet
4 Sings like a Swiss goatherder
10 Tardy
14 ___, dos, tres, cuatro, ...
15 Photographer Richard who took an iconic picture of a snake-draped Nastassja Kinski
16 Thor's father, in Norse mythology
17 "Incidentally," to a texter
18 Quaint bed covering made with swatches of leftover fabric
20 Biblical figure swallowed by a whale
22 Alphabet quintet that sometimes includes "y"
23 "___ to Billie Joe" (song where something's thrown from the Tallahatchie Bridge)
24 Internet address starter
26 "Pow! Right in the ___!"
28 Conjoined brothers Eng and Chang, literally
33 Last word of the Pledge of Allegiance
34 Serial ___ (nonmonogamous type)
35 Streetcars
39 Movie
41 Bed linen that's fitted or flat
43 Partner of Crackle and Pop
44 Reduced, as the difficulty level
46 Give ___ (try)
48 Ascot or bolo, e.g.
49 District in Oz where Dorothy meets the Lollipop Guild and the Lullaby League
52 Pavilion in a park, perhaps
55 Be scared of
56 G.I. morale booster
57 Equally awful
61 Footnote abbreviation
64 Middle East area that has been the site of repeated American military action
67 Nursery "piggy"
68 Hatcher or Garr
69 ___ faith (trusting act done without proof of benefit)
70 Possessive adjective often misspelled with an apostrophe
71 Big fusses
72 Wading birds that might be "snowy"
73 Animal that might be described with the starts of 18-, 28-, 49-, or 64-Across

DOWN

1 Eng. or soc. studies
2 "___ each life some rain must fall"
3 Municipal meeting places
4 Boated in style
5 Eggs, in ancient Rome
6 Crème ___ crème (elite)
7 Falco of "Nurse Jackie"
8 Central spots
9 Big-haired pal of JWoww on "Jersey Shore"
10 Baseball legend Gehrig
11 Barcelona bye bye
12 Diacritical squiggle that might be found over a Spanish "n"
13 Large button on a computer keyboard that's equivalent to a typewriter's carriage return
19 Four : quad :: five : ___
21 24-hr. cash dispenser
25 Media spots to raise community awareness, for short
27 Georgia and Latvia, formerly (abbr.)
28 Umpire's call
29 Pelvic bones
30 Moral code
31 Bicuspids and molars

Pancake Mix for Men

by Patrick Merrell

Copyright © Devarai GmbH

ACROSS

1 Commercials
4 Manly chin warmer
9 Dark brown, in a paint set
14 Kit-___
15 Maker of Reynolds Wrap
16 Beauty pageant headpiece
17 Fund for the golden yrs.
18 Odom in "Keeping Up with the Kardasians"
19 Remove a soda bottle lid
20 Pancake-mix for-men character?
23 ___ Jean King
24 Roadside stopover
25 Org. concerned with clean air
28 13:00, on a 12 hr. clock
29 Come down to earth
31 Country singer Jackson
32 Norway's capital
34 Accompany to a party
36 Pancake-mix for-men character?
39 Gen-xer's parent
41 Type of torch at a luau
42 Classic theater name
43 Ice rink shape
45 "The Sopranos" topic
50 Alternative to Yahoo!
51 Actress Larter or McGraw
52 Items that might be emblazoned "Soup's On"
53 Pancake-mix for-men character?
57 White House grounds barrier
59 Poked (around)
60 Place to get a massage
61 Hollywood's golden statuette
62 Bananas
63 Director Burton
64 Where a celeb might go to dry out
65 Light offense?
66 "Didn't I tell you"

DOWN

1 With hands on hips
2 Samantha's "Bewitched" husband
3 Horse "hotel"
4 Home of the Orioles
5 Gladden
6 Kroger competitor
7 Make lion sounds
8 Charles who wrote "On the Origin of Species"
9 About-face, in an auto
10 Common toothpaste flavor
11 Fellow on a "most eligible" list
12 The Reagan years, e.g.
13 Genre for Eminem
21 Swallowing sound, in the comics
22 Next to bat
26 3, 4 or 5 on the links
27 Tiny hill builder
29 Inc. cousin
30 Main artery
31 Bullet, in poker
33 Walk in the park
35 Wasn't generous with
36 Pre-packaged noontime meal
37 Poehler of "Parks and Recreation"
38 Drip on the driveway
39 Bikini top
40 Winning tic tac-toe row
44 Austrian city where Anne IV runs backwards?
46 Body part that's waved
47 Palms off
48 Where four and twenty blackbirds were baked
49 "Aw, that's ___"
51 Sharp tongued
52 "Am not!" reply
54 March Madness org.
55 Soup du ___
56 Ballpark figs.
57 In favor of
58 Suffix with legal

Critter Crooning

by Kelly Clark

Copyright © Devarai GmbH

ACROSS

1 Rip
5 Nuclear energy sources
10 "___, old chap"
14 The "I" in "The King and I"
15 Made on a loom
16 Chess ending
17 Positive response to "Shall we?"
18 Poet's muse
19 Air Force heroes
20 Elton John's reptilian stone?
23 Submarine detector
24 Sleep clinic study, briefly
25 CBS forensic series
28 Danish toy blocks
32 Spots in the sea
34 "Too cute!"
37 Captain & Tennille romance a rodent?
40 Male offspring
42 Assumed name
43 Suffix with tip, hip, or quip
44 Metallic Beastie Boy's simian?
47 Charlemagne's domain: Abbr.
48 Bone: Prefix
49 Frame job
51 Hanoi holiday
52 Tell a whopper
55 Singer Bonnie
59 Survivor's big cat's peeper?
64 Scottish hillside
66 Lake catch
67 Cairo's river
68 Merit, as wages
69 Big name in insurance
70 Rating for a program blocked by a V chip
71 Concert equipment
72 Urban hazes
73 Chair

DOWN

1 Bathroom powders
2 Juan's January
3 Playwright Chekhov
4 Scamp
5 Wowed
6 Pop singer Amos
7 White House office shape
8 Taxi ticker
9 Sound asleep?
10 Apple computer
11 Penitent's garment, Biblically
12 Had lunch
13 "Sure!"
21 City near Provo, Utah
22 Leave out
26 Break off, as ties
27 Grenoble's river
29 U.S. territory in W.W. II fighting
30 Nobel Peace Prize city
31 Rinds
33 Classic Mercedes-Benz roadsters
34 Monastery head
35 Not as good
36 OK Corral figure
38 Do an autumn lawn job
39 "Well, I hate to break up ___"
41 U-turn from NNW
45 Shoe bottom
46 Mongolian nomad's tent
50 Creates watercolors, say
53 Smidgens
54 Violinist Zimbalist
56 "Uncle!"
57 Actress Hopkins of "Family Matters"
58 "Trick" Halloween alternative
60 Urges
61 Tornado tossed pooch of film
62 Installed, as curtains
63 In-flight announcements, for short
64 "The Golden Girls" co-star of Betty and Rue
65 Ewe's mate

Top Secret

by Elizabeth C. Gorski

Copyright © Devarai GmbH

ACROSS

1 Use a phone
5 Leaf in "Leaves of Grass"
9 Sprinter's race
13 "Garfield" dog
14 River to the Baltic
15 Regarding
16 ___ Romeo (Italian wheels)
17 Pale purple
19 Beloved
20 Observe
21 Auction actions
22 "Fiddlesticks!"
24 Manhattan district with a film festival
26 Aussie greeting
27 Tennis champ Monica
28 Spray can
32 Lansbury of stage and screen
34 Hog food
35 Parisian pal
36 Outback hoppers
37 Most important
39 ___ even keel
40 Big fuss
41 "Hold it!"
42 "No Exit" playwright
44 Place for a night table
46 "The Lion King" lion
47 Like fine wine
48 Some flat-panel TVs
51 Picasso/Braque art movement
54 Groundbreaking tools?
55 Gallery display
56 Spoken
57 Long (for)
59 La Scala melody
60 Capital on a fjord
61 Oscar-winner Guinness
62 Fishing spot
63 Animal house?
64 Fragrant gift
65 Converse

DOWN

1 Seashore
2 Grace of "Will & Grace"
3 *Nas studio album of 2012
4 Meadow
5 *1984 comedy film with many sequels
6 Running shoe brand
7 Hair tamers
8 Historic period
9 Pops, to a beatnik
10 On the briny
11 Christmas tree topper
12 Honker
18 *Chuck Norris action film of 1985
21 Cow's accessory
23 Angelic instrument
25 Honey bunch?
26 Battering wind
29 *One of Columbus's ships
30 Suave Sharif
31 Queue
32 Riyadh resident
33 Protuberance
34 Command to Fido
38 Went hastily
39 Globes
41 Perukes
43 Latin 101 word
45 One who's on deck?
46 Fern seeds
49 Disney mermaid
50 Unadorned
51 Hip
52 Celestial bear
53 Island near Java
54 Saintly ring
58 Corn spike
59 Likely

"Bible Jeopardy: We're Outta Here!"

by Kelly Clark

Copyright © Devarai GmbH

ACROSS

1 Cookbook direction
5 Absolutely detested
10 Square to be avoided in Monopoly
14 Wyatt at the O.K. Corral
15 Where unborn babies develop
16 Humorist Bombeck
17 He broke all Ten Commandments.
19 The Boston Red Sox, for one
20 Forever and a day
21 Big name in pet food
22 Regal residence
24 Quit, as a job
26 Club in a Barry Manilow hit, with "the"
27 It is located in northeastern Africa.
33 Drives away
36 Grouchy Muppet
37 Water: Fr.
38 Small mountain lake
39 Photographer Adams
40 Twinge
41 Emergency PC key
42 Apple drink
43 Has the nerve (to)
44 The Book this puzzle is based on.
47 "___ have to do"
48 "___ Fables"
52 "Yes, Captain!"
55 Library ID
57 Old hand
58 Wild hog
59 The traditional founder of the Jewish priesthood.
62 Constellation bear
63 Insurance giant
64 "Well, gosh darn!"
65 Golfer's gizmos
66 Bakery supply
67 The Beatles' "___ Leaving Home"

DOWN

1 Waste conduit
2 California/Nevada lake
3 Does pressing work?
4 Sch. in Troy, N.Y.
5 Compassionate
6 Elementary particle
7 Hardy heroine
8 Poetic "before"
9 Sink's get-rid of-the garbage device
10 Trans-Atlantic air traveler's problem
11 Vicinity
12 Apple computer
13 Pretty poor, as an excuse
18 They may express relief or sadness
23 Mimic
25 "Yay, me!"
26 Roman orator of note
28 Short poem of fourteen lines
29 County of Salem, Massachusetts
30 Calendar span
31 French door part
32 Yanks
33 Dish cooked in a pot
34 Dish of leftovers
35 Killer whale
39 Corridor
40 Free ticket
42 The "C" of N.Y.C.
43 Spanish mistress
45 Toppers for pageant winners
46 Blots lightly
49 O of the magazine world
50 Lying facedown
51 Tunes
52 Lie next to
53 Time long past
54 Alleviate
55 Infinitesimal amount
56 They're often confessed
60 Part of a giggle
61 Commercials

Triple Jump

by Patrick Merrell

Copyright © Devarai GmbH

ACROSS

1 Walked (on)
5 Car loan figs.
9 Challenge
13 "___ it, boy!" ("Fetch!")
15 Burglar's haul
16 Unlocks, in verse
17 "Will ya look at that!"
18 Rodgers and Hammerstein's "The King ___"
19 They're scanned at the checkout, for short
20 Dusting for a dog
22 Scrapbook adhesive
23 Dem.'s opposite
24 Word before Comfort or Baptist
26 People with puffed packs
30 Twirled
31 Financial help
32 Sharpton and Roker
34 ___ Gump Shrimp Co.
38 Suave schemers
43 Egyptian peninsula
44 Boxer known as "The Louisville Lip"
45 ABBA's "Mamma ___!"
46 Etta in old comic strips
49 Convertible living room piece
52 Tabby tempter
56 Quick punch
57 Taxi alternative
58 Rescue teams on the slopes
63 Scrabble draw
64 Shakespearean king
65 Ragtime legend Blake
66 Not working
67 Million or billion suffix
68 Bicycle-wheel part
69 Loch with a legendary lurker
70 Lose it emotionally
71 Swarm (with)

DOWN

1 Cry at the end of a workweek
2 Toss, at the craps table
3 Gaze longingly upon
4 Go ashore
5 "There oughta be ___ against that"
6 Small lakes
7 Events with bulls and broncs
8 Roil
9 Ring that's fried and maybe frosted
10 Bobber's mouthful
11 Happen again
12 German steel city
14 Cone for a Comanche
21 TV's Winfrey
25 Big horn
26 Backtalk
27 Woman's name spelled with Roman numerals
28 Get too much of, slangily
29 ___-pitch softball
33 Place for a massage
35 Black sphere with a fuse, in cartoons
36 Soft French cheese
37 "That's ___ commentary"
39 Acorn makers
40 Stadium level
41 African golfer Ernie
42 Spanish table wine
47 Model S, Model X, and Model 3
48 Reap, as profits
50 Fortunes
51 Sudden
52 Take over mid dance
53 Put up with
54 Plays the rat
55 Pageant headwear
59 Get ready, as for surgery
60 Double-reed instrument
61 Facebook thumbs-up
62 Appear

49 Shredded
50 More lofty
54 Transmitted
55 Katie Holmes and Tom Cruise's daughter
56 Smell ___ (be suspicious)
57 Otherworldly glow
58 Common precipitation in April
59 Type of fat used in many steamed English puddings
60 ___ de Triomphe (Paris landmark)
61 Cutesy-___ (too precious by half)
62 Filbert or cashew

Mental Gymnastics

by Boris Loring

Copyright © Devarai GmbH

ACROSS

1 Side order at a diner
5 Investments for one's golden years (abbr.)
9 Urban's opposite
14 Cookie that debuted in 1912
15 Snack
16 Disease that's the subject of "The Hot Zone"
17 Appear to be
18 ___ gin fizz
19 Stitched up
20 Step up to speak at an assembly
23 Historical period
24 "Top Gun" actor Kilmer
25 "Angie Tribeca" network
28 Storage box that Geraldo Rivera erroneously hyped as full of treasure
33 Boxing's "The Greatest"
34 Paltry
35 Abject fear
36 The Soup ___ ("Seinfeld" character)
38 Chomped down on
40 Ike's partner in the candy aisle
41 Without conscious input, slangily
44 Vincent Van ___
47 Just minted
48 J.R.R. Tolkien trilogy, with "The"
51 Finale
52 Letters on a luggage tag bound for northern California
53 "That's ___ brainer!" ("D'uh!")
54 Name given to the first flag of the Confederacy
60 Sleep disorder caused by poor breathing technique
63 Monetary unit whose name suggests the continent where it's used
64 Hawaiian feast
65 18 holes in golf, typically
66 River to the Caspian
67 Great lake that sounds spooky
68 Terra ___ (baked clay)
69 Middle Eastern pocket bread
70 Rave's partner

DOWN

1 Sponsor of a dinner party
2 General vicinity
3 Search for
4 Class in which to learn the domestic arts, familiarly
5 Physically fit
6 Part in a play
7 Starting from, temporally speaking
8 Defer action on
9 Make a vow ... or a brand of carpet cleaner
10 Taxi service app
11 It's perpendicular to a column
12 Pub provision
13 Fictional collie
21 Streetcar, to a Brit
22 Kiln used in beer brewing
25 English mathematician Alan who was the subject of "The Imitation Game"
26 England chaps
27 Scatter about
28 Program for friends of Friends of Bill W.
29 Chameleon or gecko, for instance
30 Sphere
31 Sound from a horse
32 Provide weapons to
33 Type of 29 Down common in Florida
37 Implanted contraceptive such as Mirena or Kyleena (abbr.)
39 Foot's "finger"
42 Fried tortilla
43 "... long walk ___ short pier"
45 Energy bar ingredient, often
46 Fore-'s opposite, when referring to the legs on a horse

"Top(s) o' the Mornin'!"

by Kelly Clark

Copyright © Devarai GmbH

ACROSS

1 "All kidding ___..."
6 "Princess of Power" from 1980s cartoons
11 Sleep on it! :-)
14 "Rosemary's Baby" author Ira
15 Former Secretary of State Powell
16 Stars and Stripes land: Abbr.
17 "Hit 'em in the old ___" (gut)
19 Scot's hat
20 Sierra Club founder John and namesakes
21 Grew rapidly: 2 wds.
23 "Your ___" (how to address the Queen)
26 British fellow
27 Gets on the soapbox to talk
28 A bit of precipitation
31 Nickel-and ___ (that guy who piles up the "little" fees)
32 Cher's one time singing partner and husband
33 Mortgage org.
34 The Beatles' "Back in the ___"
35 Daring bikini
36 Hair holder
37 Filmmaker Spike
38 Mob scenes
39 Reward for a worker's good performance
40 Traps
42 Life's work
43 Fills to the gills
44 Ancient Egyptian king
45 Souls, to Jung
47 Dog pound sounds
48 Dove's sound
49 Witty banquet emcee
54 Seek elected office
55 Color of honey
56 Salami choice
57 Coast Guard officer: Abbr.
58 Visibly upset
59 Ms. Lauder of cosmetics

DOWN

1 Priest's robe
2 Sun. talk
3 "___ Got a Secret"
4 Line through a circle
5 Software buyer, usually: 2 wds.
6 Spine-tingling
7 "Bonanza" brother
8 Antlered animal
9 Fragrant German white wine
10 Saint ___ of Padua, patron of lost items
11 They're fluttering in your stomach when you're nervous
12 Biblical birthright seller
13 Wettish
18 Morsels
22 Gave the go ahead, briefly
23 Computer component
24 Up and about
25 Jazzy improv gatherings: 2 wds.
26 Upcoming marriage announcement
28 Tree's support system
29 "Ah, now it's clear to me": 3 wds.
30 The New York Times, The Wall Street Journal, etc.
32 Loafers and sneakers, e.g.
35 Tedious
36 Loving touches
38 Machine gun sound: hyph.
39 Run riot
41 1960s war zone, briefly
42 Serene
44 Make another effort
45 Farm measure
46 Verb preceder, often
47 Belgian river
50 Attorneys' org.
51 Explosive initials
52 Abbr. in a help wanted ad
53 Actress ___ Dawn Chong

"More Good Book Giggles (or Groaners)"

by Kelly Clark

Copyright © Devarai GmbH

ACROSS

1 Knitter's need
5 Circle segments
9 Sped
14 Olympics sword
15 After-Christmas event
16 Piano exercise
17 Cain kept up his dislike for his brother just so ___
20 King David's poetic specialty
21 First day of Lent application
22 Country road
23 Like a finished dinner
26 Broody rock genre
28 In late December, Adam blurted out: "___!"
35 Ship's director, briefly
36 Ending with "teen"
37 Muhammad's religion
38 Lincoln's nickname
39 "Golly!" in Glasgow
40 Fashion inits
42 "Do ___ say!"
43 Things you don't want to do
45 Pairs
47 Suffix with young and/or hip
48 Before Boaz got married, he was a ___ guy!
51 Ornamental Japanese fish
52 Reply to "Who's there?"
53 Where to shop
56 It might say "Welcome" on it
58 One sixteenth of a pound
62 How did Noah raise capital? Why, he ___
66 Acid in proteins
67 Cherished
68 ___ Kong
69 Like nice beaches
70 9-digit ID nos.
71 "The ___ the limit!"

DOWN

1 Kennel cry
2 Mil. addresses
3 Actress Sofer of "General Hospital" (NEAR anagram)
4 Fail to take care of
5 Pompous fool
6 "Go team!"
7 Make spotless
8 Darns a sock, say
9 Hi-___ graphics
10 Totally bewildered
11 Havana's home
12 Genesis garden
13 Remove, as text
18 Asian nurse
19 Throat-clearing sound
24 ___ II (razor brand)
25 20 x 4
27 Postal delivery
28 "___ help it!"
29 It's forbidden
30 Paid for
31 Take advantage of the demo
32 Fill with joy
33 Bouquet holders
34 Mideast leaders
39 Nobel Peace Prize city
41 Grounded soundbreakers, briefly
44 City in the San Francisco Bay area
46 Squirms painfully
47 Private detectives
49 Key ___ Pie
50 Managed care grps.
53 Degrees for painting students
54 ___ mater
55 Pork cut
57 Puts two and two together
59 Cozy corner
60 Sch. overlooking Harlem
61 Heart tests, for short
63 Delivery from Santa
64 Fleming who created 007
65 12th graders: Abbr.

"Hey There, Sugar!"

by Kelly Clark

Copyright © Devarai GmbH

ACROSS

1 School orgs.
5 Means of escape
11 Poem of praise
14 Assistant
15 Money, in slang
16 Beanie Babies, e.g.
17 One hard to fool
19 Aviate
20 Walks quietly with heels raised
21 Lads' partners
23 Summer setting in N.Y.C.
24 "I ___ vacation!"
27 It's between Mon. and Wed.
28 Foolish folks
32 Skeleton parts
35 Canonized French women: Abbr.
36 Took a chair
37 Declare openly
38 Bout of indulgence
40 "A Doll's House" heroine
41 Gridiron official, for short
42 "Star Trek" navigator
43 Piggish remarks?
44 Credit for doing something nice
48 "So that's your game!"
49 Can't carry ___ (is tone deaf)
50 Suitable
53 Bar in many a western movie
56 State cop
58 Japanese pond fish
59 "Simple!"
62 Wayside stop
63 Body of environmental regulations
64 High -tech 1982 Disney movie
65 The eldest daughter in "Little Women"
66 Adjusts, as a clock
67 Editor's "let it stand"

DOWN

1 Kindergarten adhesive
2 Shy
3 Get used (to)
4 Rockefeller Center muralist
5 Hosted, as a game show
6 Gave an unwelcome poke, informally
7 Pal of Pooh and Piglet
8 Caribou kin
9 Spinnaker, e.g.
10 Sword covers
11 Baseball player's vacation time
12 Chip's cartoon chum
13 Ice cream known as Dreyer's west of the Rockies
18 Normal state of muscle tissue
22 Seek damages in court
25 Throw into confusion
26 Contribute to the poker pot
28 Church bench
29 "Golly"
30 "They grope in the ___..." (Job 12:25)
31 Depot stops
32 Stinging remark
33 Superior to
34 "Really, I'm serious!"
38 ___ generis (unique)
39 Urgent request
40 Tiny criticism
42 Juicy-tidbit seeker
43 ___ a kind (unique)
45 A question of identity
46 Surpass in gluttony
47 How corn is planted
50 Not together
51 Black tea
52 Former senator Lott of Mississippi
53 Whole milk alternative
54 First-rate
55 Pleasant
57 Halloween mos.
60 Canon camera brand
61 The Browns, on scoreboards

Garden Parties

by Elizabeth C. Gorski

Copyright © Devarai GmbH

ACROSS

1 No longer wild
5 Vinegar-y
11 Foot rub response
14 Throat-clearing noise
15 Colombia's capital
16 ___ Lanka
17 She played Paige Matthews on TV's "Charmed"
19 Negative responses
20 Gawk (at)
21 Curvy letter
22 Considers
24 Deuce follower, in tennis
26 Windpipe, for one
27 Amy Brenneman played this psychiatrist on TV's "Private Practice"
32 Big name in athletic shoes
33 Crazy
34 NASCAR advertiser
37 Misfortunes
38 Country singer McGraw
39 A couple of laughs?
40 Victor Hugo's "___ Misérables"
41 Send forth
43 ___ back (downsized)
45 Cuban-born model who is Revlon's first Latina spokesperson
47 Brewpub
50 Sitcom star Foxx
51 "The Tempest" sprite
52 Monk's title
54 Writer of famous fables
58 Repair
59 "The Bell" novelist portrayed by Judi Dench in a 2001 biopic
62 Mao ___-tung
63 Resurrection Sunday
64 Analogy words
65 Washington D.C. VIP
66 Make a comeback?
67 Common lunch time

DOWN

1 Sailors, in slang
2 "Cat on ___ Tin Roof"
3 Southwest plateau
4 Green gemstones
5 '70s hit song by The Jackson 5
6 Persuasive, as an argument
7 Freudian topics
8 Services for stranded motorists
9 Suffix with señor
10 Halloween "treats"
11 Good ___ (repaired)
12 Bakery scent
13 ___ fit (tantrum)
18 Tragedy by Euripides
23 Goof up
25 "___ showtime!"
26 Hard-working insect
27 Colorado ski resort
28 Not busy
29 Fixes a squeak
30 Opposite of separateness
31 Pirate's booze
34 Pretzel seasoning
35 Biblical pronoun
36 Writing tablets
38 "___ the season ..."
39 Submitted, as homework
41 At a previous time
42 Hr. fraction
43 Take to court
44 Bug-repelling wood used in closets
45 Billy ___ Williams
46 Art shop worker
47 White House occupants in 1910
48 Crop up
49 One of Santa's reindeer
52 Punch deliverer?
53 Queue after Q
55 Mediocre
56 Prefix that means "eight"
57 Unit of loudness
60 "Norma ___"
61 Large coffee pot

Envious Position

by Andrew J. Ries

Copyright © Devarai GmbH

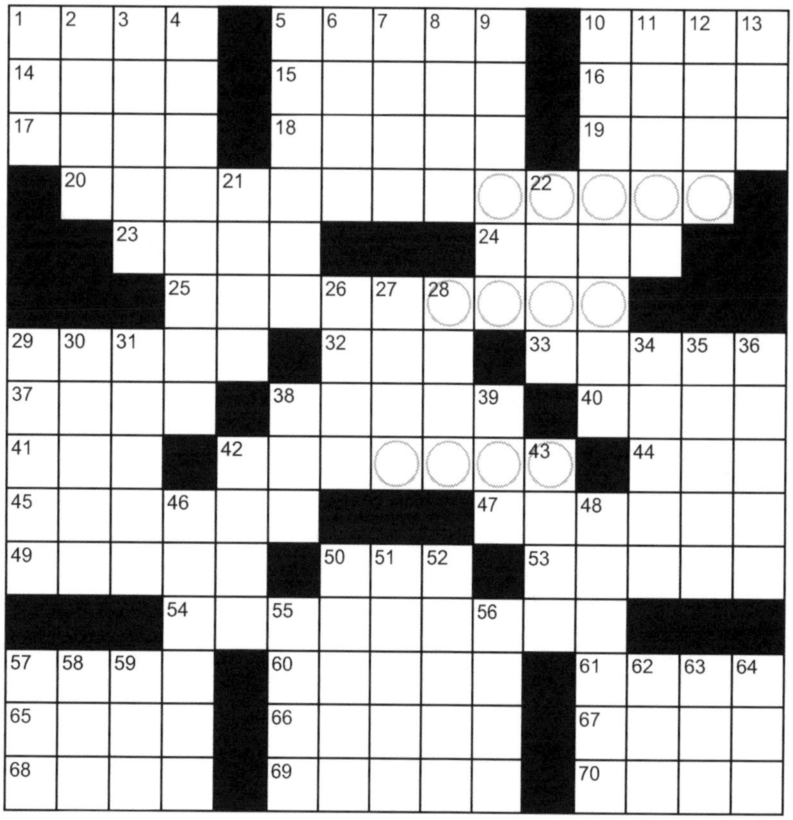

ACROSS

1 Two kings, perhaps
5 Language of the Vikings
10 Sound of blunt impact
14 Killer whale
15 Lewis Carroll title gal
16 Caped savior
17 Put points on a map
18 R & R trip, in modern slang
19 Boiling anger
20 Soap opera premiere of 1968
23 Loafer, e.g.
24 Depend (on)
25 "Can't beat that price!"
29 Secures with a deadbolt
32 Fish eggs
33 Joe of "Goodfellas"
37 Interoffice email heading
38 Milk and butter and such
40 Far from sunny, as a disposition
41 ___ Nashville (country music label)
42 Awe-inspiring
44 In the past
45 Feeling the alcohol, say
47 Rock guitarist, in slang
49 "Toodles!"
50 Pasture plaint
53 Cleans up, as text
54 Money, casually...and a feature of 20-, 25-, and 42 Across?
57 One of the martial arts
60 Not current, as a reference
61 Hooters collectively referred to as a "parliament"
65 Leave out
66 Use a pencil's end
67 One working on short orders
68 Xbox enthusiast's purchase
69 Scruffs
70 Religiously venerated

DOWN

1 Play with bubble wrap
2 Folkie Guthrie
3 Clickable array on a computer screen
4 Bad news on a power bill
5 War forces at sea
6 "Frozen" snowman
7 Kung pao side dish
8 "Git!"
9 Down-in-the dumps donkey of kiddie lit
10 On cloud nine
11 Having much weight
12 Prod
13 She's a deer
21 Auctioneers sell them
22 Avoid a rain puddle, perhaps
26 Saudi, for one
27 Gardeners spread it
28 Hatcher of Hollywood
29 Branches of a tree, e.g.
30 Exactly when expected
31 Short-lived trend
34 "Same here"
35 Bandleader Xavier known as the "Rumba King"
36 Steam implements in the laundry room
38 Firework that doesn't go off
39 Singer Sumac
42 Burn the surface of
43 Corporate muck-a-muck
46 Fertilized ovum
48 "How'm I doin'?" New York City mayor of old
50 Stiller's comic partner
51 Available from the keg, as a beer
52 Having much, much weight
55 Genesis garden
56 Gator tails seen in the soft drink aisle?
57 Run at a leisurely pace
58 Thurman of "Pulp Fiction"
59 Like lighting for romantic settings
62 Try to win over
63 Text chuckle
64 Bird's place

47 In ___ (as found, to an archaeologist)
48 Stacked, as lawn chairs might be
49 Polite denial to a lady
52 College for Prince Charles's boys
53 Fancy tablecloth border
54 Distort
57 Hairdo styled with a pick
58 Corp. money execs
59 No longer in the outbox
61 Bite a dog or down a sub
62 Madison follower on a NYC sign
63 Precious stone
64 Busy agcy. on April 15

Elephant Jokes

by Patrick Merrell

Copyright © Devarai GmbH

ACROSS

1 What do you call an elephant at the North Pole?
5 Parts of a corn plant used for making pipes
9 Canvas-prepping stuff
14 Double-reeded instrument
15 Land to the south of Ecuador
16 Statuette proudly displayed in a movie mogul's office
17 What time is it when an elephant sleeps on your sofa?
20 "Come up and ___ sometime"
21 Bao ___ (Vietnamese emperor who's name is an anagram of "aid")
22 ___ Aviv
23 Babe that baas
25 Medicare add on
27 What's gray and wears glass slippers to a ball?
33 One ___ time
34 Do in, as a vampire
35 Landlocked land abutting Vietnam
37 Scale used to measure earthquakes
39 Cool off an injury using a frozen pack
42 Arthur of tennis fame
43 Victim of an April 1st joke
44 POW/___
45 Two elephants had to share an umbrella. How did they stay dry?
50 Black and white MAD magazine characters
51 Losing tic-tac toe row
52 Golfing great Ernie
55 Some N.F.L. linemen (abbr.)
56 Computers used by many graphic artists
60 How do you fit an elephant in the refrigerator?
65 Water on either side of the U.S.
66 At any time
67 Elvis Presley's middle name
68 Amphibians whose eyes might be used in a witch's brew
69 Supporters of Obama and Hillary, for short
70 The majority

DOWN

1 Areas for parking cars
2 Off-Broadway award
3 Not all
4 Swarmed
5 USN noncom
6 Opposite of 'neath
7 Bikini top
8 Dessert that sounds like part of the weekend
9 Accompany
10 Zig-zag curve
11 Edinburgh native
12 Locked box for storing the family jewels
13 Type of hygienist
18 Least, quantity-wise
19 Wyatt of the Old West
24 ___ Stanley Gardner
25 Paper-towel layer
26 Like a shaved head
27 Model/actress Delevigne
28 Formal reply to "Who's there?"
29 "Eine Kleine ___ Musik"
30 Listening organ
31 Wynonna Judd's mom
32 Take to the repair shop, as a disabled car
36 Catch, as a stocking
38 Whacks with an axe
39 Suffix with super
40 Entice
41 Magical drink
43 Western outposts with stockade fencing (abbr.)
46 They might say "Kiss the Cook!" or "Dude with the Food" at a barbecue

Woman" star Carter

56 Fancy Japanese beef

57 Geraint's love in "Idylls of the King"

58 Turkey ___ (Thanksgiving "malady")

59 Fort rich wth gold

60 Monster in Himalayan myth

61 Retirement spot?

62 Deeply regret

Horsing Around

by Andrew J. Ries

Copyright © Devarai GmbH

ACROSS

1 Paper or plastic option at the grocery store
4 Public speaker's perch
8 Robotic sci-fi character
13 Education basics, briefly
14 Ultimately result in
16 Like kids on a sugar high
17 Pilot's approximation: Abbr.
18 Nut-yielding hardwood tree
19 More than overweight
20 Strolled by on Rodeo Drive, perhaps
23 Passover meal
24 In addition
25 Phenomenon whereby sugar pills produce positive results
33 Indie musician DiFranco
35 ___ hoop (device for gyrating)
36 Sheet of microfilm
37 "On the ___" (Jack Kerouac classic)
39 "Exactly!"
42 Org. including the Power Five conferences
43 Prides of lions?
45 Nudges on one's shoulder
47 Make a mistake
48 It hangs on rings in the bathroom
52 Day spa utterance
53 Spies may gather it, for short
56 Annual May race...whose first three finishers start 20-, 25-, and 48 Across
61 Bucking beast
63 Bills and coins and such
64 Particle studied in physics class
65 Jazzy Blake
66 Struck down, in the biblical sense
67 Cape ___ (Massachusetts resort area)
68 Good Samaritan's acts
69 One side of World War II
70 Genre that's a predecessor to rocksteady

DOWN

1 They come to a head at a bar
2 "Glee" character played by Kevin McHale
3 Liberace's was encrusted in rhinestones
4 Lone female judge described in Judges
5 From the top
6 The ___ of March (bad time for Caesar)
7 "Parting is ___ sweet sorrow"
8 Wane
9 Sashed garment
10 Needed to pay back
11 Bouncers check them
12 Hair stylist's supply
15 Instagram upload
21 "Summertime Sadness" singer Lana ___ Rey
22 "The Raven" poet
26 Baby bear
27 Whitney who invented the cotton gin
28 Swahili's language group
29 Appendage used for foreshadowing in "Jaws"
30 Extreme thinkers
31 Blacken, as chicken
32 Rip into pieces
33 Venus de Milo's lack
34 Trevor ___ ("The Daily Show" host)
38 Moisture on grass
40 Long-nosed lake predator
41 Make a choice
44 Medium gatherings
46 Verbally assented
49 Condemned house occupant, maybe
50 Pals
51 Serpent's tail?
54 Kindle download
55 "Wonder

51 Noted flag lady ___ Ross
53 Common sans serif typeface
55 Beauty queen's crown
56 Big name in extermination
57 Seriously strapped
58 Accountant's acronym
59 ___ instant (toute suite)
60 Bay Area cop's letters
62 9-digit nos.
65 The A of IPA

Just Stir

by Andrew J. Ries

Copyright © Devarai GmbH

ACROSS

1 Animal represented by Aries in the Zodiac
4 Sticks in a vase?
9 Bring to a slight boil, as milk
14 Here, in French
15 Actor Hammer of "The Social Network"
16 Group with lots of hits?
17 One shaking in their boots, say
19 Figure on an "I'm With Stupid" T-shirt
20 Doesn't bring up again, as a topic of conversation
21 "Red" fish of deception
23 Jacob's biblical twin
24 Omaha's state: Abbr.
26 Crazy way to run
27 Move laterally quickly
29 Painting or sculpture
31 Annoying audio/video mismatch
33 Like a wet blanket
36 Territory whose largest city (Nuuk) has a population just over 17,000
39 Paddler's implement
40 Delta or American fee
42 Vote against
43 Appliance brand with an eddy in its logo
45 Personal preference
47 Dubai's nation: Abbr.
48 "Long ___ and far away..."
49 Course for immigrants, for short
50 Spice blends for barbecue masters
52 Beaver's construction
54 Prestigious British prep school
58 Focus for a gym rat
61 Breathe in and out
63 Canadian native
64 Equal chance...and a description of this puzzle's circled squares
66 "Just the ___, ma'am" ("Dragnet" catchphrase)
67 Without any bells or whistles
68 Free (of)
69 Having correct pitch, as a singer
70 Low spots
71 Either of these

DOWN

1 Hunter's weapon
2 Units of rural measurement
3 Popular Mazda model
4 Anti-DWI org.
5 Attempting
6 Oscar host, e.g.
7 Farrow once married to Frank Sinatra
8 Late-night host Meyers
9 Excessive flattery
10 "Alice's Adventures in Wonderland" author Lewis
11 Language spoken by the Boers
12 Big cat at a zoo
13 Deputy ___ (canine TV toon)
18 Maker of the Rodeo
22 A picky one is tough to cook for
25 Burgers, wings, and such
28 Very, very picky
30 Not imagined
32 Pesky insect
33 "___ hear this!"
34 Honolulu's island
35 Religious pal of Robin Hood
36 Pirate's cocktail
37 Tools for catching butterflies
38 Salon stock
41 "Not for me," at the bridge table
44 Bring back together, as old friends
46 First Hebrew letter
49 "Bam!" celebrity chef

Silence of the Lams

by Harvey Estes

Copyright © Devarai GmbH

ACROSS

1 Off your rocker
6 Chowder type
10 Self-satisfied
14 Muscular strength
15 Jay once of late night TV
16 Spare in the trunk
17 MacDowell of "Groundhog Day"
18 Divisible by two
19 Right on a map
20 Japanese buyers club?
23 Senate spots
24 "WKRP" actress Anderson
25 Take away
28 Lend a hand
29 "Be prepared" org.
32 "Star Trek" counselor Deanna
33 ___-frutti ice cream?
35 Canon camera brand
36 Noisy music competition?
40 Work on a stage
41 Rub the wrong way
42 High point
43 Comfy shirt
44 NFL 6-pointers
45 Great wealth
47 Channel for a tear
49 Part of a party's platform
51 "South Pacific" summons for overactors?
55 Ken of "Brothers & Sisters"
56 Cop's regular route
57 Cerebral output
59 ___ the Hyena of "Li'l Abner"
60 Cheery tune
61 "Go for the ___"
62 One-time spouses
63 Bombeck of "At Wit's End"
64 Didn't take part, with "out"

DOWN

1 New York Knicks org.
2 Coffee containers
3 "I did it!"
4 Bathing trunks, e.g.
5 "I'll be right there!"
6 Chin dimple
7 Big name in jeans
8 Once again
9 Monument in "2001"
10 Beer glass
11 Florida vacation destination
12 Big Dipper bear
13 Escape, with "away"
21 Granola bar bit
22 Foster of "Panic Room"
25 Chance to get a hit
26 Knee protector
27 Where to sign
28 ABA member
30 French river to the English Channel
31 Long-eared beasts
33 Quite a bit
34 Mysterious blip on the radar
37 Gate fastener
38 Furniture piece by the sofa
39 Went in reverse
45 Tried to get elected
46 Deep blue
48 Forearm bones
49 Poem of King David
50 Led Zeppelin's "Whole ___ Love"
51 "Jeopardy!" host Trebek
52 Golda of Israeli politics
53 "___ la vie!"
54 Winslet of "The Reader"
55 "Stick that bull!"
58 Grass section

I-Test

by Victor Fleming

Copyright © Devarai GmbH

ACROSS

1 Healing indicators
6 Rush order letters
10 Eject, as lava
14 Old Testament scroll
15 Old Italian bread?
16 Swampy area
17 Type of navel
18 Stalker's object
19 Mean sort
20 "I ___" (Barry Manilow)
23 Story start?
24 Vegetable that rolls
25 Roar of approval
26 Scheduling abbr.
29 Clip again, as a hedge
31 Fancy duds
33 Hawk family member
37 Learn of
38 "I ___" (Muhammad Ali)
42 Two-tone cookie
43 "Return to ___" (Presley tune)
44 Toddler, slangily
47 Blocked, as a river
51 Incoming flight info
52 Gun enthusiasts' org.
54 Trophy, at times
55 Store in a cask, say
56 "I ___" (Lynn Anderson)
60 Jet black stone
62 Guesser's phrase
63 Lines on a pie chart
64 Info
65 Lone Star St. school
66 Haircut discard
67 Hold to be
68 Sailors
69 "Fiddler on the Roof" matchmaker

DOWN

1 Overhead compartment user, say
2 Dinner segment
3 Oil producer
4 Minnows, often
5 Timid
6 Letter before beta
7 "Your majesty"
8 Comeback to "Am not!"
9 Disc jockey's bribe
10 Grimy air
11 Nasty places
12 Miscalculate
13 Quite small
21 The Sun Devils' city
22 Fishbowl accessory
27 Tantrum thrower
28 ___ Lingus
30 Helicopter part
32 Unit of heat
34 Some NFLers
35 Before, in poems
36 Japanese currency
38 In ___ (stuck)
39 Computer memory unit
40 Total
41 Event for Alice
42 Rough stuff
45 "The Ice Storm" director ___ Lee
46 Go for a spot on the team
48 Drive up the wall
49 He's full of himself
50 ___ Huxtable (Lisa Bonet role)
53 It's located just above the heart
54 Farm produce
57 Crammer's worry
58 ___-friendly
59 Beef order
60 Unmatched, as socks
61 Not, to a Scot

date ___ Paul
56 Dove's murmur
57 Subject of a high school cover-up?
58 Ctrl + ___ + Del
61 Furious anger
62 Pocket item for a golfer
63 Put in the microwave, in slang

On A Roll

by Andrew J. Ries

Copyright © Devarai GmbH

ACROSS

1 Step on a banana peel
5 ___ diem (Latin phrase meaning "seize the day")
10 Gives a visual scan
14 Right-hand person
15 "___ Gold" (1997 "bee" movie?)
16 Top worn on casual Friday, maybe
17 One might be on a roll
20 When repeated, gung-ho
21 Sean Lennon's mother
22 Bill on which George Washington is front and center
23 Cheap start?
25 U-turn from WSW
26 Not the quiet type
28 Wrap in a gyro joint
30 Lifesaver, e.g.
31 One might be on a roll
36 Tinder success
37 Title prison for Solzhenitsyn
38 Alternative, in Spanish 101
40 Option for planning for the golden years
41 Christmastime payouts, for some
43 Corn unit
44 Fashionista Lauder
46 College senior's undertaking, for short
47 "Siddhartha" author Hermann
49 "The Tank Engine" of kiddie lit
51 Fractions equal to around 16.7%
52 One might be on a roll
56 Russian leader of old
59 Coke, to Pepsi
60 Big name in snack crackers
64 Difficult to keep a grip on
65 Unlikely venue for an indie rock concert
66 Length times width, for a rectangle
67 "The Simpsons" bus driver with a palindromic name
68 Red-headed fast-food eponym
69 Ooze

DOWN

1 Buffalo hockey player
2 Purple flower
3 Crop from the Gem State
4 Chest muscle, for short
5 King title mutt
6 "Go jump in ___!" ("Buzz off!")
7 Intel-gathering mission
8 Black tea variety
9 "College GameDay" airer
10 Org. with clean air standards
11 Walking the dog may be part of it
12 Justice Kagan
13 French philosopher Georges
18 Japanese city and namesake of an international treaty
19 Adored to pieces
24 Three squared
27 Black-and white sweet treat
29 2012 Ben Affleck thriller
30 Gigantic
31 Overly mean
32 Participated in a choir
33 Speak drunkenly
34 Give a shock
35 Empty wrappers, rotted food, e.g.
36 Plan for intake?
39 Greek god of war
41 Guy going a courting
42 LaBeouf of "Lawless"
45 Beginning stage of life
48 There are many spotted in a war movie
50 It's stuck in a malt
51 Spread (out)
53 Grow weary
54 Like 2, 4, 6, or 8
55 2016 candi-

It's Coming

by Victor Fleming

Copyright © Devarai GmbH

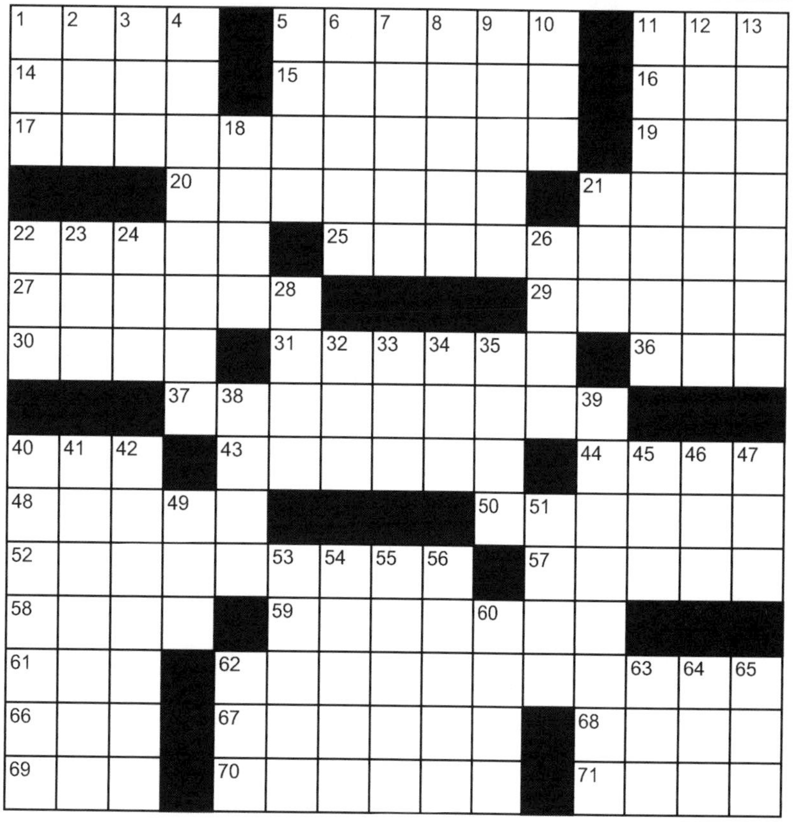

ACROSS

1 Wedding cake layer
5 Square and circle
11 Swampy ground
14 Explorer of Nickelodeon
15 Lyric-forgetter's cover
16 "Feliz ___ nuevo"
17 Taken unawares, say
19 Catch sight of
20 Like some athletes
21 Cow-headed Egyptian goddess
22 Spud variety
25 Something that's destined to become popular
27 In a bigger way
29 Volkswagen model
30 Netman Sampras
31 Mason of "The Goodbye Girl"
36 Street sealing matter
37 Words needed to complete 17-, 25-, 52-, and 62 Across
40 Perfect, at NASA
43 Dealer's demand
44 Face cover
48 Test period
50 Small canine herder
52 2009 Brad Paisley song
57 Stand up
58 Look like a creep?
59 Almost out of gas
61 The ___ (British rule in India)
62 In a state of readiness, say
66 ___-Caps (movie candy)
67 Paparazzo's need
68 Et ___ (and others)
69 Yo-yo or Slinky
70 Most underhanded
71 School in New Haven

DOWN

1 NFL six-pointers
2 Debtor's note
3 Hit the wrong button, say
4 Listing of prior offenses
5 Lose weight, with "down"
6 ___ coming (deserves to be punished)
7 Hebrew alphabet opener
8 San Diego ballplayer
9 Nudge with an arm bone
10 Verbalize
11 Droopy-eared hound
12 The tiniest crumb
13 Is quite successful.
18 Olds classics
21 "So ___ heard"
22 Mischievous sort
23 Female deer
24 Gallery collection
26 Not completely shut
28 Sign of 37 Across
32 Fore's partner
33 Have regrets about
34 Good name for a diner cook
35 Cadence calls
38 Saintly ring
39 Totally common
40 If all else fails
41 Italian dressing spice
42 Stick-in-the mud
45 Manning of the Giants
46 Part of FWIW
47 Caustic soap-making compound
49 Part of a royal flush
51 Really dislike
53 Fable takeaway
54 Military adversary
55 Home made of hides
56 Bradley and Epps
60 Start to fall?
62 Gateway products
63 State with keys (abbr.)
64 Italian dressing ingredient
65 "Norma ___" (Sally Field movie)

neighborhood fort
62 Mia of women's soccer
64 What a rabbi might walk into, in a joke

Dog Show Groups

by Patrick Merrell

Copyright © Devarai GmbH

ACROSS

1 Popular Apple computer
5 Places offering mud baths and massages
9 "Hammer" used to restore order
14 Kunis of "Ted" and Jim Beam ads
15 "... why ___ thou forsaken me?"
16 Oyl with a brother named Castor
17 Deserted locale scouted for "Survivor"
18 Pretentious
19 Dreaded "leave" in bowling
20 Little green men in a kid's room
23 South African golfing great Ernie
24 Woody Guthrie's boy
25 One, in Deutschland
27 Money for use in day-to-day business operations
34 Iranian tongue
35 Suffix with planet
36 Game that involves galloping on grass
37 Ruckus
38 Home-grown residents
42 "This minute!"
43 Chicken of the Sea offering
45 Uncle, grandfather or husband
46 Meat cuts above flanks
48 Reasonable shot at winning
52 Flavor-enhancing ingred.
53 "___ I a stinker?"
54 Winter hrs. at Disneyland
57 Broken-check textile pattern
63 "I was out of the country," for one
65 The bubble part of a bubble bath
66 Prefix before legal in a legal office
67 Pertaining to the moon
68 Falco of "The Sopranos"
69 One in an express aisle count
70 Brainy
71 Monopoly proof of purchase
72 Subject with a lab, for short

DOWN

1 "You're looking at the whole department"
2 Japanese soup
3 Wartime partner
4 ___ Palace (casino)
5 "Do you want me to?"
6 President's "get out of jail" grant
7 Sparking Italian wine
8 Eyelid affliction
9 Grapevine fodder
10 Swiss peak
11 Nasty
12 Like villains
13 Allows
21 Terminix competitor
22 Duane ___ pharmacy
26 A touch of the sauce
27 Crumple
28 Maine college town
29 Start of an auctioneer's warning
30 Western ___ (history class, briefly)
31 Common gin mixer
32 Friendless
33 Daily temperature extremes
34 Name before Domino or after Minnesota
39 Helpful hombre
40 Sunburn alternative
41 Reporter's angle
44 Hand holder?
47 To the point
49 Skateboarder's top, often
50 Club lugger
51 Warned, as a snake might
54 Chums
55 Poor area of town
56 Palin impersonator Fey
58 On a thrift store rack
59 Many a classic painting
60 Swear words allowed in court
61 Place for a

"That Takes The Cake!"*

by John M. Samson

Copyright © Devarai GmbH

ACROSS

1 Loose ones sink ships
5 "Champion" of Spain
10 Three, in Tijuana
14 "___ for All Seasons" (1966)
15 "Whoopee!"
16 This spot
17 Topsy-turvy*
19 Falco in "The Sopranos"
20 Even considering
21 New England prep school
23 Shirt part
24 Emerald Isle
25 Tennis ranking
27 Radar of "M*A*S*H"
30 Shop cleaner, briefly
33 Tavern chair
35 "Fiddler on the Roof" hero
36 Sonic boomerang
38 Cargo bays
40 Vaccines
41 Valerie Harper role
43 Lively dances
45 Pothole filler
46 Turns into
48 ABBA ballerina
50 Prophetic sign
51 "Old Blood and Guts" general
55 Gives in
58 Molify
59 Piece in a blind
60 "Baloney!"*
62 Mark a ballot
63 Less congenial
64 Surveying nail
65 Wharf
66 Tall and thin
67 Spine-chilling

DOWN

1 Praises
2 Urge forward
3 Not in vogue
4 Shoots from ambush
5 Canines that bite
6 Take on cargo
7 Chang of Hogwarts
8 Hawkeye State
9 One of Santa's reindeer
10 Conjectures
11 Santa Claus suit material*
12 One of the Great Lakes
13 Clairvoyant
18 Seedy bars
22 Dr. Atkins's plan
26 Places for buzzers
27 Of time past
28 The Harp constellation
29 One Earth orbit
30 Action word
31 Aspirin target
32 Labrador color*
34 World Cup cheer
37 Mileage instrument
39 Like wet roads
42 Church corner
44 Ginger cookies
47 Call for
49 "Relax, soldier!"
52 Brownish gray
53 Award for "Moonlight"
54 Down and out
55 Invitation letters
56 "The Time Machine" good guys
57 Humane org.
58 Supermodel Wek
61 John Cena win

52 Pipsqueak
53 Detests to the core
56 Improve, as skills
57 Ronny's Mayberry character
60 They're not from 51 Across
62 Pod veggie

Brain T's-ers

by Andrew J. Ries

Copyright © Devarai GmbH

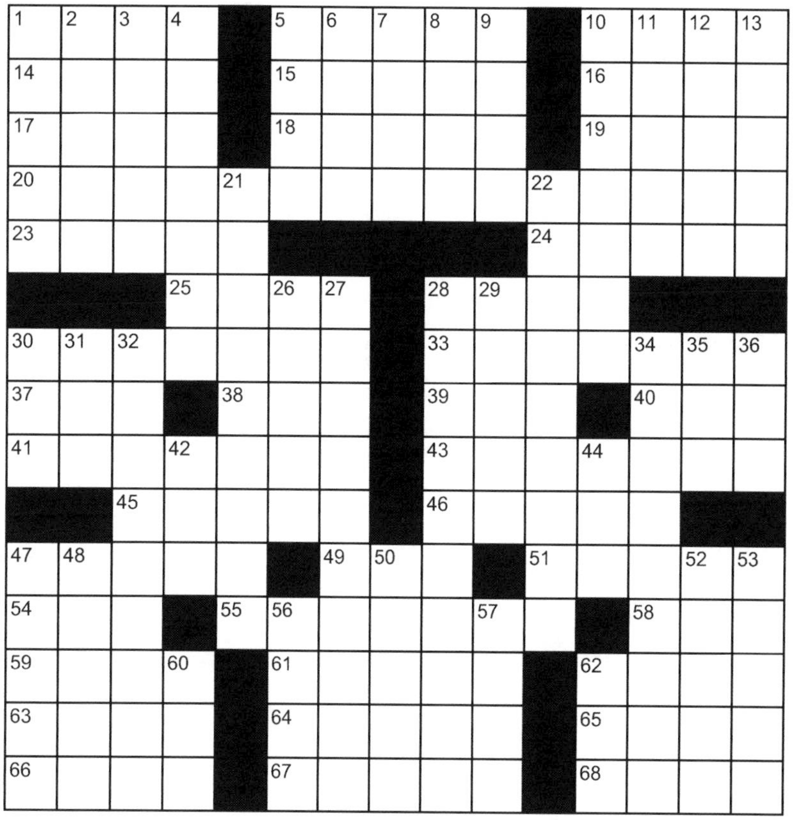

ACROSS

1 Arachnid's creations
5 Daily delivery
10 Pepsi, e.g.
14 Instrument used in Guinness' logo
15 Get out of the way
16 Wilson of "Midnight in Paris"
17 "And others," in footnotes
18 Like billiard balls numbered one through eight
19 Small faults
20 "Dancing" idiom evoked in dubious transactions
23 Shorthand professional, for short
24 Urge, as with a cartonful of Grade-As?
25 Do a housekeeping chore, or the target of that chore
28 Russian ruler of old
30 Carrying tragic consequences
33 Race hosted at a marina
37 Memorable period of time
38 Bad start?
39 Hoppy choice in a beer garden
40 Give a hand
41 Tell a 23 Across what to write
43 Pittsburgh stealers?
45 On the periphery
46 Soup spoon
47 Opportunity for a barista's artistry
49 ___-kwon do
51 ___ Day (mid April observance)
54 Yours and mine
55 Blake named People's Sexiest Man Alive in 2017
58 Former flier
59 "That's correct"
61 Yellow primrose whose name includes an animal
62 One working with iambs and stanzas
63 "The art of making a point without making an enemy," per Isaac Newton
64 Oscar-nominated Watts
65 French 101 verb
66 Poses a question
67 Lauder seen in the cosmetics aisle
68 Biblical biters

DOWN

1 Uses a stone to sharpen
2 Patronize a restaurant
3 It's stepped on to stop
4 Equal alternative
5 Flyswatter's target
6 State openly
7 ___ Alto, Calif.
8 Cut a paragraph or two, perhaps
9 Complete from the beginning
10 Food giant whose brands include Parkay and Peter Pan
11 Attributing (to)
12 "Take your hands off!"
13 Williams of "Happy Days"
21 Lovers who were made for each other
22 Floral spot for taking an afternoon cup
26 Pricey roof material
27 Lone Star State city named for a U.S. president
28 Tempo of many a waltz
29 Brown-colored Instagram filter option
30 Government agent, briefly
31 Bush press secretary Fleischer
32 Mobile restaurant well stocked with tortillas
34 Cyndrical side option at a burger joint
35 NFL rarity
36 YouTube annoyances
42 Egyptian "boy king"
44 In the manner of
47 "Whole ___ Love" (Led Zeppelin classic)
48 Warm glows
50 Divvy out

parts
48 Practices public speaking
49 Word in arctic forecasts
50 Nebraska's largest city
52 Like some "The Biggest Loser" contestants
53 After-dinner candies
56 Non-thinking one
57 Netflix competitor
58 Bagnold who wrote "National Velvet"
61 "Take a load off"
63 Sis's sibling

Colorful Rhymes

by Andrew J. Ries

Copyright © Devarai GmbH

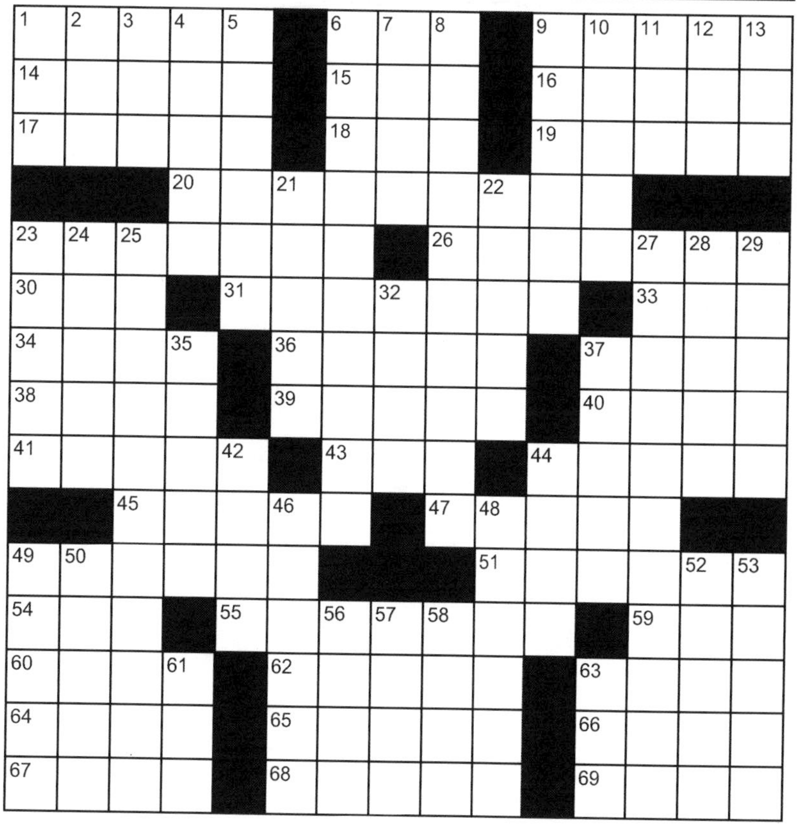

ACROSS

1 Samuel ___ Boston Lager
6 One getting paid to play
9 Gives the go ahead
14 Smart set
15 ___ Claire, Wisc.
16 "Yup"
17 One-named Greek new age artist
18 Singer DiFranco
19 Running total
20 Colorful rhyming card game
23 Soft drink roll out of 1985 that was a marketing disaster
26 "Fine, fine..."
30 Barbeque residue
31 Words that attempt to settle down a growling dog, maybe
33 ___ Speedwagon
34 Hot topic in 2010s geopolitics
36 Kerfuffles
37 Maker of the Genesis video game console
38 Nixon's nixing power
39 Solo opportunities for opera singers
40 Unwanted garden growth
41 Use, as force
43 The P of MPH
44 Strong and virile, stereotypically
45 Hangs on to
47 They have knobs and hinges
49 Japanese art form of growing small trees
51 Ben and Jen flick, e.g.
54 One-time Capitol Records parent
55 Colorful rhyming "carrot top"
59 Bringing a teammate home gets you one
60 Annoying Netflix problems
62 Dracula's title
63 "Where have you ___?" (concerned parent's question)
64 Surprised greeting
65 "Love Me Like You Do" singer Goulding
66 It recharges one's batteries, so to speak
67 Light bulb unit
68 Important beams when hanging drywall
69 Singles for a bartender, maybe

DOWN

1 Comedian Schumer
2 Org. concerned with traffic
3 ___ Arbor, Michigan
4 "Morning Joe" airer
5 The Commodores hit set at sea
6 Volunteer program established in 1961
7 Compile a Top Ten list, maybe
8 Occult object used at a seance
9 Public protest, e.g.
10 Neutral shade of some slacks
11 Puck org. that's not quite the big show
12 Brynner of "The King and I"
13 Like one who's hardly the life of the party
21 Curly-tailed dog breed
22 "I'm at ___ for words"
23 Believing pigs fly, say
24 Southeast England county
25 Colorful rhyming hero
27 Colorful rhyming film set backdrop
28 Philosopher Georg
29 One sucking up to a boss
32 Musician Brickell
35 Leper's multitude
37 Horde of bees
42 Turn a ream of paper into confetti
44 Overall attitude
46 Jigsaw puzzle

"Visual Aids"

by Kelly Clark

Copyright © Devarai GmbH

ACROSS

1 French romance
6 Stinging flier
10 Doorpost
14 Al ___ (pasta specification)
15 Cube maker Rubik
16 Arab ruler
17 Bundle of wheat
18 Slanted type: Abbr.
19 Common cat food flavor
20 Fortified wine holders
23 Anatomical pouch
25 One side in checkers
26 Marsh growth
27 Circle of good friends
32 Love to pieces
33 Designed for flying, briefly
34 Conks on the head
35 Dwelling place
37 Early Michael Jackson hair style
41 Ode or haiku
42 Mistake
43 Contractor's guidelines
47 Whacks with an open hand
49 Early U.S. nuclear org.
50 Pop the question
51 Examine carefully (and this puzzle's theme)
56 Kitchen fixture
57 Aptly named citrus fruit
58 Dormitory units
61 Unlikely prom king candidate
62 German denial
63 Letter-shaped fasteners
64 "Slow Churned" ice cream brand
65 Heredity carrier
66 The Devil

DOWN

1 Commercials
2 "Hardly overwhelming"
3 Modest ice cream cone order
4 Bryce Canyon state
5 Boxing match official
6 Eccentric one, slangily
7 Pretentiously cultural
8 Minor setback
9 Public opinion assessment
10 High-flying socialites
11 Tickles
12 Dug for gold
13 Military bigwigs
21 TiVo remote button
22 West Coast gas chain
23 Natural wound protector
24 Designer Gucci
28 Grads to be: Abbr.
29 Ruth's mother in-law
30 Rocker Nugent
31 "___ we having fun yet?"
35 "You've Got Mail" ISP
36 Sleep on it
37 Dadaism founder
38 Completely lose it
39 Enormous birds of myth
40 Russian city on the Ural River
41 Galileo's birthplace
42 Former Ford compacts
43 Where to buy a birthday cake
44 Overturns
45 Chuck Berry title girl
46 Hair goo
47 Slingshot missile
48 Took a bath
52 ___-ho (very enthusiastic)
53 S-shaped molding
54 Hollywood's Ken or Lena
55 "Game of Thrones" actress Chaplin
59 N.Y.C. subway overseer
60 Nine-digit ID

59 Sinking ship's signal
62 Sunbeam

Opposite Beginnings

by Patrick Merrell

Copyright © Devarai GmbH

ACROSS

1 Female titles that are contractions
6 Start of an underling's title (abbr.)
10 Tells white lies
14 Musical key that cyclists don't like?
15 Rubber ducky's locale
16 Elevator inventor
17 University of Maine town
18 "Hmm, interesting"
19 Bone parallel to the radius
20 Broadening one's horizons
23 Home appliance giant
24 Dr. of daytime TV
25 Swedish pop group
28 The Buckeyes' sch.
31 Like a play that has no breaks
35 Susan of "The Partridge Family"
36 Prayer-ending words
38 West married to a Kardashian
39 Directly preceded out the door
42 Amazed by
43 Felt miserable
44 Bradstreet's credit-rating partner
45 Stereotypical artist hats
47 "The Tell-Tale Heart" author
48 Harry Truman's wife
49 Presliced bread purchase
51 Beaver coverer
53 Away, with a goal in mind
59 Lover's quarrel
60 Two-person performance
61 Mooer's milker
63 "Yeow!"
64 Subj. in art or med school
65 Marketplace of ancient Greece
66 Onetime Atl. Ocean crossers
67 Title for Godiva and Chatterley
68 Bad, bad Brown of song

DOWN

1 Little Red Book author
2 Hairdo that's picked
3 Felipe or Jesus of baseball
4 "Om" is a common one
5 Showing no emotion
6 "Nowhere Man" lyric: "Isn't he ___ like you an me?"
7 Cloth belt
8 Like some San Francisco streets
9 "Pinball Wizard" group
10 Lucky type of clover
11 "There, there, ___ be okay"
12 Sticky situation
13 Org. that issues monthly checks to retirees
21 Actress Watts
22 Made piggy sounds
25 Go off script
26 Designer Geoffrey
27 Overwhelmingly
29 Sonic the Hedgehog co.
30 Like a nerd
32 "+" battery terminal
33 Miley or her dad, Billy Ray
34 Years preceding the big 2-0
36 "Am not!" comeback
37 Normandy battle town that's an anagram of "lots"
40 What a calendar is divided into
41 Gripes
46 Footwear in a Biblical epic
48 Suspension or draw follower
50 Flora's counterpart
52 Typical
53 Numbered musical work
54 Undisputed statement
55 Big name in school notebooks
56 Start of a phrase meaning teeny
57 Air freshener's target
58 Fiddling emperor

Devarai CROSSWORDS

Puzzle 87
www.devarai.com

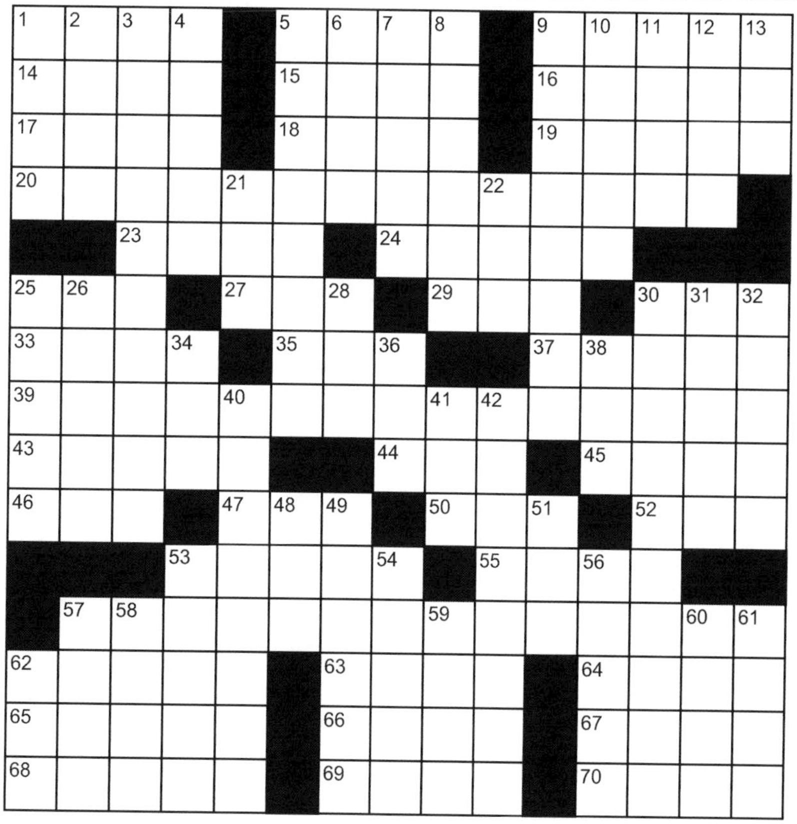

Geezer Superheroes

by Patrick Merrell

Copyright © Devarai GmbH

ACROSS

1 Maker of explosive tennis balls and dehydrated boulders
5 Ran, as ink
9 Not once
14 Calendar heading abbr.
15 Swamp
16 Live
17 Type of Japanese soup
18 '80s H.S. grads
19 Their homes might be made of paper or mud
20 Geezer superhero
23 Michael of "Juno"
24 Gown
25 Give in to gravity
27 Play a role
29 Biblical verb ending
30 Stomach muscles, briefly
33 Painter's calculation
35 Eternity
37 Bread specification at a deli
39 Geezer superhero
43 Late
44 Emulate a rug
45 Pair of walkers
46 Metal-bearing rock
47 Mendes of "Training Day"
50 Damage, as a surface
52 Snider of Twisted Sister
53 Online currency
55 Ladder part
57 Geezer superhero
62 Line dance of Cuban origin
63 Hawaiian party
64 Genie's home
65 Attempt to get
66 Mil. org. providing White House helicopter transport
67 Factual
68 "___ blame you one bit"
69 Have a rendezvous
70 Advantage

DOWN

1 Convenience store conveniences
2 One that's dipped in dip
3 Rock, classical or rap
4 Wear away
5 Self-propelled dirt track equipment
6 Schreiber of "Salt"
7 Made mistakes
8 Hunger
9 Local TV offering at 6:00 and 11:00
10 Tests
11 Passport stamp
12 Channel in a sports bar
13 A.C.L.U. concern
21 Geologic division
22 NBA hanger on?
25 Took care of
26 Noisy, as a stadium
28 Remove a disabled car
30 Brink's truck worker, for example
31 How scotch might be categorized
32 Touch, smell or hearing
34 Put numbers together
36 Org. with games played on thin ice
38 Lon succeeded by Pol Pot
40 Optometrist's wall hanging
41 Goal
42 Opening for a crybaby
48 Brewing vessel
49 Political safe haven
51 Pirate's drink
53 Prod
54 Green Monopoly purchase
56 Nick of "Hotel Rwanda"
57 State of mind
58 Data
59 Pathetic
60 Obnoxiously superior
61 Olympic event for Ivan Osiier from 1908 to 1948
62 Film special effects, for short

Going the Distance

by Elizabeth C. Gorski

Copyright © Devarai GmbH

ACROSS

1 Toothpaste types
5 Sonar sounds
10 Some plasma TVs
14 Z ___ zebra
15 Eric Clapton hit
16 "Sleepless in Seattle" director Ephron
17 Box lunch?
19 Hard fat used in bird feed
20 Celebration that involves food
22 Away from SSW
23 Tony-winning "horse" play
25 River mouth formations
27 "Law & Order" spinoff, initially
28 Quarterback's throw
31 Curved line on a musical score
32 "Homeland" spy gp.
33 Pig's nose
35 ___ out (intimidate)
38 "Give this ___!" ("Taste!")
40 Country singer Tucker
42 Squirrel's home
43 Actress O'Neal of "Paper Moon"
45 Contented cat sounds
47 World Cup cheer
48 Qatar's ruler
50 Splendor
51 The Braves, on scoreboards
52 Team self-esteem
54 Enjoys a book
56 Charged particle
57 The "E" of EU
61 Penny loafer, for example
63 "Wheel of Fortune" finale
67 Tennis match divisions
68 Occurrence
69 Zwei follower
70 Citrus drinks
71 Twiggy homes
72 Panache

DOWN

1 Driving need?
2 Atty.'s title
3 "Elementary" actress Lucy
4 Major mix-up
5 Enjoyable
6 Pet food brand
7 Russian refusal
8 Delighted
9 Leafy side dishes
10 ICU workers
11 1971 James Taylor hit with the lyrics "Take to the highway ..."
12 Rock concert venue
13 Fills fully
18 Stays on for another stint
21 Website with restaurant reviews
23 Patti LuPone Broadway role
24 Musical symbol
26 A deadly sin
27 "Shoo!"
29 Shower bar?
30 The crack of dawn
34 Beginner
36 Ancient Britons
37 Pointy stiletto shoe part
39 Arizona tribe
41 Airplane seat separators
44 Marathon fraction ... and it's the puzzle theme!
46 Asparagus unit
49 Sandwich made with sauerkraut
52 Beethoven's "___ Solemnis"
53 ___ and aahed (expressed amazement)
55 Battery terminal
58 Wander freely
59 Tip jar bills
60 Football kick
62 Winding road shape
64 Web address initials
65 PBS funder
66 Loud racket

54 Bug with its own season?
55 Yang's counterpart
57 "Eat ___ chikin" (Chick Fil-A cow's cry)
58 Penultimate Greek letter
59 Salt Lake City native, once

Get A Clue!

by Sam Ezersky

Copyright © Devarai GmbH

ACROSS

1 Slinky's shape
5 "Big" WWI gun
11 Angry Birds or Fruit Ninja, e.g.
14 "___-daisy!"
15 Hawaiian greetings
16 "The Matrix" protagonist
17 Freshwater fish with a colorful scale pattern--did this one do it?
19 "Shut yer ___!" ("Be quiet!")
20 Get in a trap
21 It's a free country
23 What Hester Prynne wore, in literature-could it be this person instead?
28 Teenage dreams?
29 Put ___ on (limit)
31 Fib--perhaps she committed the crime?
36 Church singing group
37 Went back for seconds and thirds, say
38 Decontaminate
40 Face-to-face exams
41 "Boulevard of Broken Dreams" hit-makers-maybe this guy?
42 Editor's mark for removal
43 Give a signal to
45 Item ripped then squeezed on a hot dog, maybe--is he the guilty one?
51 Bares fruit?
52 Pot-___ (French stew)
54 "Just so ya know," in texts
56 Traditional Christmas dessert--this man did it, now it's time to figure out the weapon and room!
60 Jeremy of the NBA
61 "Please help me with directions"
62 Fashion designer Cassini
63 Game with Skip and Reverse cards
64 Sweetums
65 Tennis match divisions

DOWN

1 Bra components
2 Uncorks
3 Jacob and Esau's father, in the Bible
4 Stretchy swimsuit synthetic
5 What a Breathalyzer measures: Abbr.
6 Yellowstone mammal
7 Burgle
8 "___ be the day..."
9 Some diner side orders
10 Liability's opposite
11 Momentarily
12 Vegetable in a pod
13 One of the Rice Krispie Treats mascots
18 "___ the rам-parts we watched..."
22 Salt Lake City resident
24 Stitch's Disney pal
25 Make the change?
26 Closed-___ shoes
27 Mikhail Gorbachev's wife
30 Zebras, to lions
31 "___ you think I was?"
32 Part of a Muslim palace
33 Humphrey Bogart's "High Sierra" co-star
34 Gay, writer?
35 Chicago trains
36 Average grade
38 Blood's gang rival, in LA
39 "Love Me or Leave Me" singer Horne
41 HS diploma alternative
43 Request after providing a phone number
44 Villain in "The Little Mermaid"
46 Lukewarm
47 Scoundrel
48 High praise
49 Submit a tax return over the Internet
50 Palindromic principle
53 Popular sheepskin boots

Funny Girls

by Kelly Clark

Copyright © Devarai GmbH

ACROSS

1 Coffee break snack
6 ___ Piggy
10 Fair-minded
14 Higher up than
15 Billing statement abbr.
16 Aware of
17 Electrician, at times
18 Furniture chain founded in Sweden
19 Elementary particle
20 "Ha ha, `Some Like It Hot Actress' ___!"
23 Attorneys' org.
25 Poem of praise
26 Clean air org.
27 Increases
28 "Ha ha, woman played by Joan Crawford and Kate Winslet ___!"
32 Leer at
33 Knight's title
34 Susan of "L.A. Law"
35 Pastoral poem
37 Puppy's bite
39 Pilotless aircraft
43 Norse war god
45 "Mamma ___!"
47 Music-playing Apple
48 "Ha ha, female disciple of Jesus ___!"
51 Opposite of WNW
53 "I Like ___" (1952 campaign slogan)
54 Droop
55 Family room, often
56 "Why am I laughing at 20, 28, and 48 Across?"
60 Scouting outing
61 Crucifix letters
62 "If ___ Hammer"
65 Jazzy Fitzgerald
66 The Laurel of Laurel and Hardy
67 Tea sweetener
68 Orbison, Rogers, and Wilkins
69 Short dogs, for short
70 Motif

DOWN

1 Margery of a nursery rhyme
2 Kimono closer
3 "As a rule..."
4 Eye layer
5 Intense fear
6 Like most absentee ballots
7 Nasty, in slang
8 Play's opening
9 Ready for the post office
10 Rivers of comedy
11 "Not so!"
12 Posture problem
13 Weighty books
21 Bad day for Caesar
22 Propelled a boat
23 Mine, in Marseille
24 Nickname for Dallas
29 Atlanta-based airline
30 ___ ballerina
31 Ritchard who played Hook on Broadway
36 Like much poetry
38 Footballs, informally
40 Essay section of a newspaper
41 All's opposite
42 Biblical plot?
44 Cracker brand
46 West who played Batman
48 In a lamblike way
49 Treating maliciously
50 One lacking proper respect for elders?
51 Old-time knockout gas
52 1970 Neil Diamond hit
57 Affirmative votes
58 Pull an all nighter before an exam, say
59 "No way!"
63 Leave it to beaver?
64 "What ___ the odds?"

"The Inside Track"

by Kelly Clark

Copyright © Devarai GmbH

ACROSS

1 Hipbone-related
6 Sail holder
10 Tailor's line
14 Milan's La ___ opera house
15 Wings: Lat.
16 Humdinger
17 Fess up (to)
18 Horror film staple
19 Circle parts
20 A.A. Milne favorite
23 Wall St. debut
25 Quadrennial games org.
26 ___ room (place for a Ping-Pong table)
27 Settle a debt
28 "If it's not here, it must be ___"
32 ___ B'rith
33 Edinburgh exclamation
34 ___ Paulo, Brazil
35 Barrio babies
37 Scottish cap
39 Choo-choo
43 Type
45 "___ Abner"
47 Advantage
48 "Can't find anybody who can handle this"
51 Dove's sound
53 Cake making recipe instruction
54 Samuel's teacher, in the Bible
55 Hospital trauma areas, briefly
56 Going places...or another title for this puzzle
60 Waikiki wingding
61 "Voila!"
62 Arson or blackmail, e.g.
65 A ___ apple
66 Airline to Tel Aviv
67 Blacksmith's block
68 Arid
69 G.O.P. rivals
70 Christmas songs

DOWN

1 "Patience ___ virtue"
2 TV screen option, for short
3 1972 feminist hit by Helen Reddy
4 Et ___ (and others)
5 Tabby's treat
6 Pulling a rabbit out of a hat, say
7 Soothing succulent
8 "No Exit" playwright
9 Giggles
10 React to an unwanted pass, maybe
11 France's continent
12 Major maker of soda cans
13 Overly sentimental
21 ___ contendere (court plea)
22 Razzle-dazzle
23 Library ID
24 Corn cake
29 "Old MacDonald" refrain
30 Hopscotch player's need
31 Tender spots
36 Replay speed
38 Important nutrients
40 Sticky stuff
41 Borodin's prince
42 Part of CNN
44 Made booties, maybe
46 "Damn Yankees" vamp
48 "That's cheating!"
49 Breathe out
50 Certain neopagan
51 Coke and Pepsi
52 Helpful
57 Melody
58 Dutch cheese
59 Rubik who invented the Rubik's cube
63 Plastic bag thickness
64 Ernie in the World Golf Hall of Fame

54 Tony's gal at the Copacabana, per Barry Manilow

56 Mambo king Puente

58 Chignon or French twist, e.g.

59 Fraternity's kegful

60 Smell ___ (be suspicious)

62 Two of them are in a qt.

63 Average guy?

"Let's Frolic"

by Boris Loring

Copyright © Devarai GmbH

ACROSS

1 Nutmeg spice ... or a self-defense spray
5 Esprit de corps
11 "Like, totally great, dude"
14 Wilson of "You, Me and Dupree"
15 Blood disorder that causes fatigue
16 "Honest" presidential nickname
17 Louella Parsons's rival in the gossip trade
19 Convent resident
20 Sharply inclined
21 Person, place, or thing
22 Goes bad
23 Having the skills
25 "Project Runway" judge and fashion designer Zac
27 ___ the pot (create trouble)
30 "___ tree falls in the forest ..."
32 Time to hit the playground in grade school
35 ___-pah band
36 Clobbered, biblically speaking
38 St. Pete's neighbor in Florida
39 Nautical job of Gilligan's boss Jonas Grumby, played by Alan Hale, Jr.
42 "I'd like to buy the world ___ ..." (line in a classic soft drink jingle)
43 Action franchise starring Liam Neeson
44 Prefix for "angle" or "cycle"
45 "A Tale of Two Cities" hero Charles
47 Edge
48 Church song
49 Scottie dog or top hat, in "Monopoly"
51 "The __ in God's Eye" (sci-fi novel)
53 Talon
55 Actor Jared of "Dallas Buyers Club"
57 The "A" in the "ABC Islands"
61 "Gr8 joke!!"
62 Common uniform for a parochial school girl
64 The entirety
65 Body ink
66 Notion
67 Memorial Day month
68 Shemp or Curly, for example
69 Civil wrong that sounds like a pastry

DOWN

1 Inventor of a mineral hardness scale
2 Mad as ___ hen
3 Yield
4 Make precious
5 ___-jongg
6 How flamingos commonly stand
7 Auctioned vehicle, often
8 Boost, as sound
9 Bank that holds a mortgage, for example
10 Unit of corn
11 Kept going despite total exhaustion
12 Be contiguous to
13 Lions' lairs
18 Cops' "be on the lookout" alert (abbr.)
22 Summary
24 Outline
26 Take hold, as fatigue
27 "Too bad, ___" (sarcastic expression of sympathy)
28 Scarpia's killer, in a Puccini opera
29 Everlastingly
31 In armed conflict
33 Type of whale
34 Lethal chemical weapon
36 Skulk
37 Breed used to pull a sled
40 "Got it"
41 ___ Sabe (the Lone Ranger, to his friend)
46 Chew out, loudly
48 Solitude-seeker
50 "Nifty!"
52 Letter between sigma and upsilon
53 Mollusk that's the epitome of happiness, in a saying

"Let's Play Post Office!"

by Kelly Clark

Copyright © Devarai GmbH

ACROSS

1 Uneasy feeling
6 Kennel cry
10 Shrinking Asian sea
14 Synagogue scroll
15 Cream additive
16 Explorer Hernando de ___
17 Cognizant
18 Russian revolutionary Trotsky
19 Vagrant
20 Conan O'Brien succeeded him on "Late Night"
23 Promise to pay, briefly
25 Oath taker's words
26 The people in the pews
27 Police department's stated goal
32 White House chief, initially speaking
33 "The Thin Man" canine
34 Gardener's spring purchase
35 Desert haven
37 Actress Lena of "Chocolat"
41 Monopoly or Scrabble
42 Pig
43 Enjoy premium service on a jet
47 French romance
49 Tire filler
50 "The Addams Family" cousin
51 "Your Majesty," for Queen Elizabeth II, e.g.
56 Heavy reading?
57 Scored 100 on
58 Extremely long times
61 Distinctive flair
62 Put on the market
63 Craze
64 "Darn!"
65 Leaves home?
66 Women's suffrage leader ___ B. Anthony

DOWN

1 ___ loss for words
2 Right this minute
3 One with a diploma
4 Poet Teasdale
5 1963 Elizabeth Taylor/Richard Burton drama
6 "Cat ___," 1965 Jane Fonda film
7 On the safe side, at sea
8 Cheer (for)
9 Superman's alter ego
10 Guru's habitat
11 Dormmate
12 Facing the pitcher
13 Bonkers
21 Tokyo, once
22 Director Kazan
23 AOL and others
24 Native Nebraskan
28 Dirt after rain
29 Stun gun
30 Forensic TV drama with multiple spinoffs
31 A.C.L.U. concerns: Abbr.
35 Buffoon
36 "___ my brother's keeper?" (Genesis 4:9)
37 Symbol of wisdom
38 Intermediaries
39 M.I.T. part: Abbr.
40 Hatchling's home
41 Greek sandwich
42 Roller-coaster shrieks
43 Arrangement
44 Light units
45 Horse rider's seat
46 French shooting match: Anagram of IRT
47 Before's opposite
48 Money, in slang
52 Speedy
53 Taiwan-based computer maker
54 Remove, as text
55 Junior posthumously inducted into the Football Hall of Fame
59 Actress Vardalos of "My Big Fat Greek Wedding"
60 ___ Francisco

Chopping Blocks

by Elizabeth C. Gorski

Copyright © Devarai GmbH

ACROSS

1 Lunch hour
4 Raised, as horses
8 Actress Mason of "The Goodbye Girl"
14 State tree of Rhode Island
16 "No need to explain"
17 Board leaders
18 Artistic asset
19 Shoot for
20 Tarzan's "commuter line"
22 Links org.
23 "___ Bovary"
25 Mozart's output
27 Flounder's kin
30 Hold dear
32 Swiss canton
33 Snow day coaster
35 Early automaker
36 Web-address starter
38 Rx for Parkinson's
40 Sundance Festival's home
43 Docile
45 Some cameras (Abbr.)
47 Greek vowel
48 Villain of Spider-Man
51 Navy bigwig
53 Blood line?
54 A choir may sing in it
56 Pirate's guzzle
57 Bedazzle
58 Olympic skater/gold medalist Ilia
62 B vitamin
65 Mocking
67 Dead giveaway?
68 Valued, as a colleague
69 Jazz vocalist ___ Bridgewater
70 Suffix with team or young
71 Ninny

DOWN

1 Killer whale
2 Soda pop brand
3 Wax-coated cheese
4 Pub bills
5 Turntable speed meas.
6 Lifted up
7 Overall material?
8 Wee parasite
9 Khan title
10 Seminary subj.
11 "Cinderella" character
12 Martina of tennis
13 Fasten
15 Where the Dolphins play
21 Japanese computer company
24 More ho-hum
25 "Blood Father" star Gibson
26 Language in Pakistan
27 "Say what?"
28 Works at a museum
29 Puppy's sibling
31 Squirrels away
34 Two, in Acapulco
37 Treaty
39 Least fancy
41 ___ glance
42 Evil computer
44 NYC transit org.
46 More hazy
48 Brought in, as a salary
49 Thelma's film buddy
50 "Shoo!"
52 Not vacant
55 Some Rodin subjects
57 Old-style dagger
59 Peru's capital
60 Currier's partner
61 Sneakers since 1916
63 Scoundrel
64 Mineral suffix
66 GPS suggestion

man numerals
62 Simple card game
64 Architect I. M. ___
65 Dug stuff

Final Authorities

by Andrew J. Ries

Copyright © Devarai GmbH

ACROSS

1 Star of many viral videos
4 Casual pants fabric
9 Where LA is, for short
14 "___ Maria" (mass hymn)
15 Toil and trouble
16 Decrease intensity
17 Sports team with a flaming basketball in its logo
19 They're expected
20 Spread on a charcuterie board
21 Make cuts to
23 Provo or Orem resident, e.g.
26 Veggie in a pod
27 Computer giant
30 "___ and the City"
31 CBS procedural set in Honolulu
35 Out of control
36 Four-door cars
37 Killer whale
40 Evenings, in ads
42 Slangy name for one's parents, with "the"
43 Cocktail made with scotch, vermouth, and bitters
45 Bar regular?
47 Dark amber colored metal
49 Fuel for the road
52 Game, ___, match
53 When repeated, a nickname for pop singer Swift
54 Make a choice
56 Bobby who hit the "Shot Heard 'Round the World"
60 Poet Khayyam
61 Goofy type
63 Sting and others
66 Spy novelist John le ___
67 Go through the door
68 Vardalos or Long
69 "Two and a Half Men" co star Jon
70 Iconic riveter
71 The Beatles' "___ the Walrus"

DOWN

1 College facility
2 Get high?
3 Levy that played a big role in the American Revolution
4 Tai ___ (meditation method)
5 "That's a laugh!"
6 Currier and ___
7 Biblical helmsman
8 Eight-armed sea creatures
9 U.S. capital founded by Spanish colonists
10 Clarinet's cousin
11 It's all fun and games
12 Backup option at a cash-only business
13 Good name for a weight loss guru?
18 "So-so"
22 Puts back into theaters, perhaps
24 "I've got it!"
25 Device that watches the watchers
28 Crook
29 A rolling stone doesn't gather it, so it's said
32 Xbox rival
33 Misbehave
34 "American ___" (reality show rebooted in 2018)
35 Painter Chagall
37 Spheres
38 What a Broadway hopeful hopes for
39 Juice source for some flashlights
41 Mind reader's "skill"
44 Month of a beer fest, in German
46 "___ you kidding me?"
48 Source of pearls
49 Twins in astrology
50 Thorny shrub
51 Small river
55 Texter's chuckle
57 Roll call response
58 "This looks bad"
59 Hockey targets
61 700, in Ro-

59 Floral necklaces
61 Jessica married to Justin Timberlake
62 Circus barker
64 Thurman of "Pulp Fiction"

No Botter

by Andrew J. Ries

Copyright © Devarai GmbH

ACROSS

1 Common dog name
5 Relating to sound
10 Deal with, as adversity
14 Use a napkin
15 ___ acid (protein component)
16 Verbally sparring, say
17 "Madagascar" lion
18 Substance that's poured into a bundt pan
20 Repressed, with "up"
21 Had the answer
22 Evidence of a sound sleeper?
23 Watch face
25 Letters preceding an alias
26 Respond to medication, perhaps
31 Historian's interest
35 Gospel singer Studdard
36 Place guarded by eunuchs
38 Green casserole morsel
39 Knock down a peg
40 Wayfarer's resting place
41 Array on a computer screen
43 Picked thing
44 Hockey playing surfaces
46 En ___ (as a whole)
47 Hang on to
49 Style of English beer similar to a pale ale
51 Tattoo artist's "canvas," often
53 Lenovo competitor
54 Houston ballplayer
57 Climactic word for an auctioneer
60 Huge amounts, in slang
63 Cosmetic lotion component
65 Mayberry redhead
66 Restrained
67 Disastrous 2017 hurricane
68 Perlman who played Carla on "Cheers"
69 French fashion magazine
70 Visibly stunned
71 Give a holler

DOWN

1 Do a little tit for-tat
2 Laundry room accumulation
3 Free exchange of ideas
4 Garment industry output
5 Angler's equipment
6 Muscat's land
7 "Just Do It" company
8 From the start
9 Toss leisurely
10 Kitty's time out
11 Headphones wearing "Simpsons" character
12 Port city's structure
13 To be, in French
19 Offer, as a price
24 Li'l guy drawn by Al Capp
25 "You ___ So Beautiful" (Joe Cocker ballad)
26 Good name for a hot dog salesman?
27 Jazzman Blake
28 Yours, in the King James Bible
29 Loses on purpose, in slang
30 ___ & Young (accounting giant)
32 The difference between "its" and "it's"
33 Taste or touch, e.g.
34 Stunning weapon
37 Try to copy
42 "Jeopardy!" selection
45 "Big Blue" in the world of technology
48 Procession with floats
50 Unfair judgment
52 Be a thief
54 Tennis legend Arthur
55 Silverstein who wrote "The Giving Tree"
56 Show and ___
57 One way to go to a party
58 ___ vez (another, in Spanish)

Let's Make It Formal

by Patrick Merrell

Copyright © Devarai GmbH

ACROSS

1 Showy neckwear
4 Say
9 Beachfront
14 It's stuffed in a sleeve
15 Who lives in a ghost town, usually
16 About half of prom outfits
17 Keanu's "The Matrix" role
18 Formal name for a groundhog?
20 Vehicle thats legal for underage drivers
22 How many Asian entrees are served
23 Desertlike
27 Highest point
28 Formal name for a hot sandwich?
32 In this spot
33 Inundated
34 ___-Wan
37 Year-end quaff
40 It might become a stub
42 High-protein bean
43 "___ luck!"
47 Many a Saudi
48 Formal name for a hand slapping game?
51 Jacob's twin
54 Louvre contents
55 Early Ford
57 Character whose heart was two sizes too small
61 Formal name for a fence topper?
65 Paris thirst quencher
66 Pandora's boxful
67 Some sodas
68 Wolf Blitzer's employer
69 Word after Home or Office
70 Write using 140 characters or less
71 Tapped container

DOWN

1 Word on a gag gun's flag
2 Double-disked dunker
3 Run ___
4 Open a gift, e.g.
5 Like Alfred E. Neuman's grin
6 In addition
7 Bring to a close
8 Abbr. on a camcorder
9 Lee who created The Hulk
10 "Yippee!"
11 Flower that sounds like an animal part
12 Volleyball star Gabrielle
13 New Jersey or English county
19 "No fooling"
21 Colorado resort
24 Double-platinum Steely Dan album
25 Compete in a regatta
26 ___ last resort
28 Females
29 Building block brand
30 Unrestrained revelry
31 ___ Beta Kappa
34 Gumbo ingredient
35 Pelican part above a pendulous pouch
36 "Can ___?"
38 Suffix with pay or schnozz
39 Succeeded, to a fair degree
41 Saguaros and such
44 Prefix with cycle
45 Something to atone for
46 It's point value in bridge is 4
48 American Indian communal structure
49 "You don't have to convince me"
50 Take into custody
51 Put in a post, as a YouTube video
52 Dry Italian wine
53 Leaking
56 With none to follow
58 What a cervical collar supports
59 Prop for Mr. Peanut
60 Installed, as a door
62 Play a role
63 "Zounds!"
64 "Like"-minded politician?

High Chair Quintet

by Elizabeth C. Gorski

Copyright © Devarai GmbH

ACROSS

1 Double-___ sword
6 Lab fluids
10 Glitz partner
14 "Chain Gang" songwriter Sam
15 New Mexico art center
16 "___ Rock"
17 Trousseau holders
19 "Hollaback Girl" singer Stefani
20 Hockey's Bobby
21 Hip-hop's West
22 Little hopper
23 Lower than, on a map
25 Motorist's "Move it!"
26 Dance syllable
27 Classic theaters
29 Great service?
32 Keyboard exercise
35 Bucking horse
36 Fish stick?
37 TV mogul Winfrey
38 "Anthem" writer Rand
39 Casino order
41 Zodiac butter
42 Set aside (for)
44 "Breaking Bad" star Cranston
45 Superlative suffix
46 Stead
47 Yosemite grazer
48 Tell-___ (revealing memoirs)
50 It's hot stuff
54 Sky boxes?
56 Sacred book of Islam
57 Possess
59 Jazzy James
60 Like Molly Brown
62 Black, in verse
63 Farrow and Hamm
64 Dog-___ (worn)
65 Some August babies
66 Eyelid woe
67 "___ show biz!"

DOWN

1 Canyon sound
2 Entrances
3 Give up amateur status
4 Squeeze (out)
5 Yuletide carol
6 Short-term employee?
7 "Yeah, right!"
8 Memory method
9 Ninny
10 Lively baroque dance
11 Backyard celebration
12 Prayer ender
13 Oodles
18 "Funny!"
22 Sunbather's tote
24 Bruins' sch.
25 London's Big ___
28 Nanny's warning
30 Very deep sleep
31 Paradise
32 Achy
33 IRS employees
34 Bit of body art
35 Hay unit
40 Annoys
43 Fleur-de-___
47 Abba of Israel
49 Depends (on)
51 Happen
52 Hooded snake
53 Baby hooter
54 Sailboat stabilizer
55 "Let ___" (Beatles hit)
56 Make a sweater
58 Rorem's namesakes
60 Sounds of indecision
61 Sigh of relief

Quickie Thinking

by Elizabeth C. Gorski

Copyright © Devarai GmbH

ACROSS

1 Tango moves
5 Bakers' measures (Abbr.)
9 Actress Mazar of "Younger"
13 West Coast sch.
14 Give a job to
15 It takes the cake
16 Top number crunchers?
19 Teeny
20 Price-less?
21 "Jane Eyre" star Wasikowska
23 Bones in forearms
24 Tragic king
25 Small coffee containers
26 Courage
27 One who eats and runs?
29 "For ___ a jolly ..."
30 Sings without words
31 Slender nails
32 Kosovo native
33 Ireland
35 Film trophy
38 Lewd material
39 Parisian Mrs.
42 Bettor with no secrets?
45 "To ___ not ..."
46 Crash, with "out"
47 After dark, in Dijon
48 English dynasty
49 Tolkien tree man
50 Target of a joke
51 Curry spice
52 Treatment regimen for a fanatic fan?
56 Jug handles
57 "Apollo 13" org.
58 In ___ (even)
59 Position on a roster
60 Future MBA's exam
61 Hatchling's cry

DOWN

1 Grant knighthood to
2 "Cool" eye color
3 Grievances
4 Yuletide workers in red suits
5 Yon folks
6 "Go get 'em, Fido!"
7 Declare openly
8 French painter Georges
9 Shower attention (on)
10 First lady
11 Dangerous "Triangle"
12 Wishy-washy
17 British verb ending
18 Foam ball brand
22 "___ Death" (Grieg elegy)
23 "This tastes awful!"
24 Gentle soul
25 Iowa crop
27 Bear hair
28 Notice of departure?
30 Basil or thyme
32 Lost buoyancy
33 Give off, as light
34 Wish undone
35 Leak slowly
36 Dishwashing aids
37 New York's ___ Park
38 Winter Olympics squad
39 Serve as referee
40 Marshmallow filled snack
41 Mess up
43 "Movin' ___" ("The Jeffersons" theme)
44 Class trip
45 Unjust verdict
48 Day before Wed.
50 Upper-body sculpture
51 Light conversation
53 Grenada gold
54 Airport screening org.
55 Opposite of "nope"

Shouldn't That Be Plural?

by Patrick Merrell

Copyright © Devarai GmbH

ACROSS

1 Barroom scuffle
6 Metric weight
10 Lancaster or Reynolds
14 Women's name that's an anagram of DAILY
15 Taboo thing, to a toddler
16 River of W.W. I
17 Dental hygiene tubeful?
19 U.S. disaster relief org.
20 Bird stomachs
21 Camel refueling stop
22 Lots of
25 Do neatener?
28 ___ last resort
29 "Spring ahead" hrs.
30 Wall St. debut
31 Rapper with the most watched YouTube video ever
32 Kayak relative
34 France's neighbor across the Pyrenees
36 Pair resting on the nose?
40 Spread outward
41 Two times
44 Commotion
47 Driving visibility impairer
48 Passats and Rabbits, for short
50 Place to pet a pig, perhaps
51 One following a conversation from afar?
54 Stitched together
55 Buccaneer's buddy
56 Pass, as a law
58 Anthony's radio partner
59 What a person leaves in the sand?
64 It's a gas in Times Square
65 Taunt
66 Blazine
67 The first James Bond film
68 Regretted
69 F-sharp equivalent

DOWN

1 Crunchy sandwich, briefly
2 Wheat alternative
3 Fruity drink
4 Broom rider
5 Cowardly Lion portrayer
6 Bother incessantly
7 Martini's vermouth partner
8 Tiny home invader
9 Head Stooge
10 Overwhelmingly
11 Depletes
12 Neglectful
13 Like third-rate novels
18 Oom-___ (tuba sounds)
21 Some woodwind players
22 Cheese-covered pasta
23 Sea-to-shining sea ctry.
24 Song-and dance stick
26 Kelly of morning TV
27 Places to get a mani-pedi
29 Cook in hot oil
33 Yiddish plaints
34 Crafty
35 Marketing word with an exclamation point, in a burst
37 ___ gin fizz
38 "Lady" known for once wearing a meat dress
39 Dress tag number
42 Grazer with an udder
43 Seemingly endless wait
44 Nut in some candy bars
45 Crib wear
46 Possibility
48 Blew off steam
49 Rolled-up deli offering
52 "I ___ other alternative"
53 Tractor brand
54 Stilted
57 Climber's handhold
59 His last V.P. was HST
60 Loire liquid
61 Nothing
62 Preceder of la la
63 Prepared

Zero Shades of Grey

by John M. Samson

Copyright © Devarai GmbH

ACROSS

1 "Yesterday" vocalist
5 Snow White ate a poisoned one
10 Degrees for mgrs.
14 Source of teen angst
15 Snowmobile route
16 Fanning in "Maleficent"
17 Yukon capital
19 Lord's wife
20 Colonized
21 Louisiana's state bird
23 A, in Berlin
24 Squid spray
25 Patron saint of Milan
29 Supercharged
33 Garage attendant
34 Carnival peep show
36 "___ matter of fact ... "
37 "Zounds!"
38 Osprey's fishhook
39 NCO Club members (abbr.)
40 Sinbad's bird
41 Banner phrase
42 Clown pole
43 Sean Lennon's mother
45 Royal residences
47 "Dude!"
48 Development parcel
49 Kitchen scrubbers
53 Twiddle one's thumbs
57 Maple seeds
58 1600 Pennsylvania Ave building
60 "Tootsie" actress Teri
61 Red lab dye
62 Patricia in "Hud"
63 Murray of tennis
64 Jet engine sounds
65 Jets grounded in 2003

DOWN

1 Furry feet
2 Aspirin target
3 Part of BTU
4 Achieved in school athletics
5 Capital of Greece
6 Give a nudge
7 Pebble Beach score
8 Have trouble with S's
9 "Waiting for the Robert ___"
10 Muslim holy city
11 Witchcraft
12 ___ mater
13 Observed
18 "Adam Bede" novelist
22 It forms at the end
25 "And ___ fine fiddle had he ..."
26 Nearsighted cartoon character
27 Classroom sight
28 Muse of lyric poetry
29 What unwatered plants do
30 Craving
31 Basketry fiber
32 Throws out a net
35 Space bar neighbor
38 Weight for bricks
39 Subway stops
41 Synthesizer name
42 Laziness
44 Cantankerous
46 Wormhole travelers
49 Long story
50 Think ahead
51 Washstand pitcher
52 "Vamoose!"
53 Recipe directive
54 Club collection
55 Prelaw exam
56 They're caught in pots
59 "Life ___ cabaret old chum ..."

Puzzle Solutions

On the following pages you find all the solutions to the crosswords.

Puzzle 1

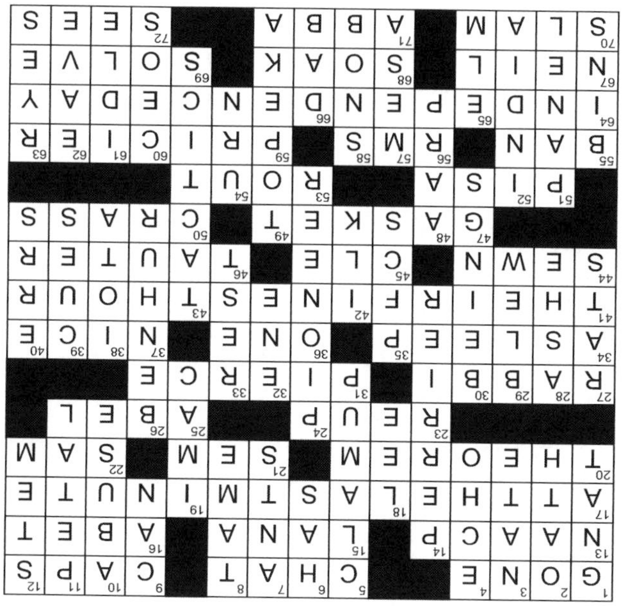

Puzzle 2

Puzzle 3

Puzzle 4

Puzzle 5

A	D	S	■	■	E	P	I	C	■	S	H	A	R	I
L	I	E	S	■	B	A	N	A	■	M	A	Y	A	N
B	A	C	O	N	B	I	T	S	■	O	W	E	N	S
E	N	T	R	Y	■	L	O	T	T	O	■	A	D	O
E	A	S	E	L	S	■	■	R	A	T	T	Y	■	■
■	■	R	O	M	A	N	O	C	H	E	E	S	E	■
S	A	D	■	N	O	S	E	■	■	S	A	S	H	A
T	R	I	G	■	G	I	V	E	S	■	R	I	O	S
A	T	S	E	A	■	■	E	M	I	R	■	R	O	T
B	E	A	N	B	U	R	R	I	T	O	S	■	■	■
■	■	P	L	A	Z	A	■	■	S	O	M	B	E	R
M	A	P	■	L	I	N	G	O	■	M	O	O	R	E
E	I	E	I	O	■	C	A	N	D	Y	C	O	R	N
T	R	A	I	N	■	O	G	L	E	■	K	N	O	T
E	E	R	I	E	■	R	A	Y	S	■	■	S	R	S

Puzzle 6

H	A	T	S	■	S	E	E	M	■	P	A	I	R	S
A	B	R	A	■	O	R	C	A	■	E	L	S	I	E
M	O	U	N	T	C	O	O	K	■	G	L	I	D	E
S	U	E	■	I	C	I	■	E	D	A	S	N	E	R
■	T	R	I	B	E	C	A	■	E	S	E	■	■	■
■	■	G	E	R	A	R	D	B	U	T	L	E	R	■
A	S	C	O	T	■	■	M	A	T	S	■	E	A	U
D	O	O	R	■	B	L	O	B	S	■	C	A	S	T
A	L	I	■	A	L	T	I	■	■	D	A	R	T	S
M	I	N	N	I	E	D	R	I	V	E	R	■	■	■
■	■	■	A	R	E	■	E	N	A	C	T	E	D	■
B	E	D	S	I	D	E	■	S	L	O	■	M	O	I
A	R	I	S	E	■	M	E	T	E	R	M	A	I	D
T	I	N	A	S	■	I	G	E	T	■	E	I	N	E
S	N	O	U	T	■	T	O	P	S	■	A	L	G	A

Puzzle 7

J	O	G	S	■	T	E	S	T	S	■	T	W	A	S
F	L	E	A	■	A	C	U	R	A	■	M	O	S	T
K	E	L	L	Y	G	R	E	E	N	■	I	M	S	O
■	■	■	S	A	T	U	R	A	T	E	■	A	O	L
I	N	S	A	N	E	■	■	D	A	V	I	N	C	I
S	E	T	■	K	A	R	L	■	■	E	L	I	■	■
A	I	R	■	S	M	E	A	R	■	L	I	N	D	A
A	G	E	S	■	S	A	G	A	S	■	E	G	O	S
C	H	E	E	K	■	L	E	V	E	E	■	O	N	T
■	■	T	A	E	■	■	R	E	A	M	■	L	E	E
S	Y	S	T	E	M	S	■	■	S	P	A	D	E	R
N	A	M	■	P	A	T	R	I	O	T	S	■	■	■
A	L	A	S	■	J	O	H	N	N	Y	C	A	S	H
K	I	R	K	■	O	N	O	N	E	■	O	V	E	R
Y	E	T	I	■	R	E	S	O	D	■	T	E	A	S

Puzzle 8

C	A	L	F	■	R	E	E	F	■	R	A	I	S	E
O	D	E	R	■	A	U	R	A	■	E	R	W	I	N
P	O	W	E	R	G	R	A	B	■	P	E	O	N	Y
A	B	I	D	E	■	■	S	R	I	L	A	N	K	A
Y	E	S	■	D	I	M	■	I	C	E	■	■	■	■
■	■	■	M	O	D	E	L	C	I	T	I	Z	E	N
H	A	L	O	■	E	M	U	■	■	E	R	O	D	E
A	L	I	T	■	A	O	R	T	A	■	I	O	N	S
S	E	A	T	O	■	■	E	O	S	■	S	T	A	T
H	E	R	O	S	A	N	D	W	I	C	H	■	■	■
■	■	■	■	T	I	E	■	N	A	H	■	L	E	D
D	E	T	E	R	R	E	D	■	■	I	R	E	N	E
E	C	O	L	I	■	S	O	N	I	C	B	O	O	M
C	O	N	I	C	■	O	M	E	N	■	I	N	T	O
K	N	I	S	H	■	N	E	O	N	■	S	E	E	S

Puzzle 9

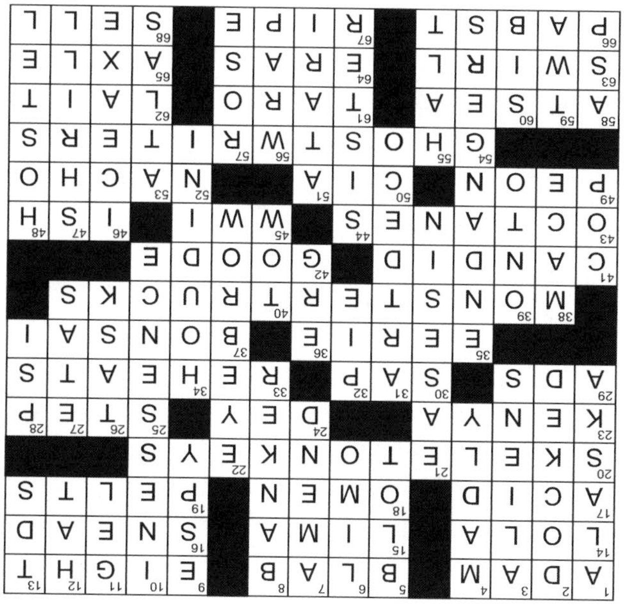

Puzzle 10

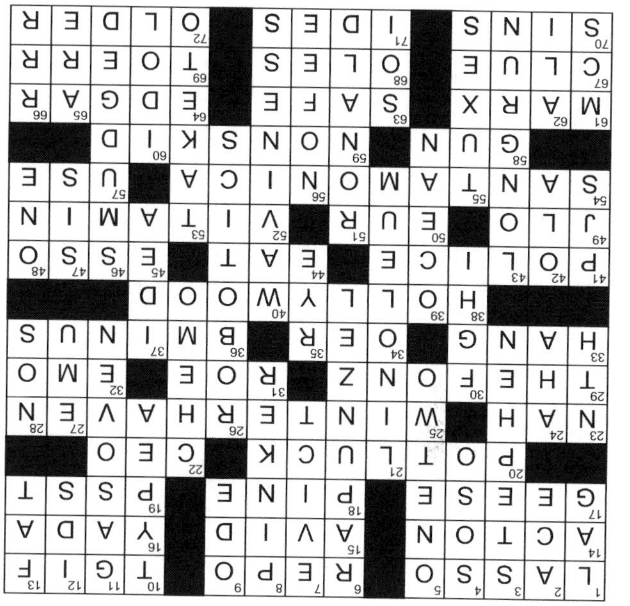

Puzzle 11

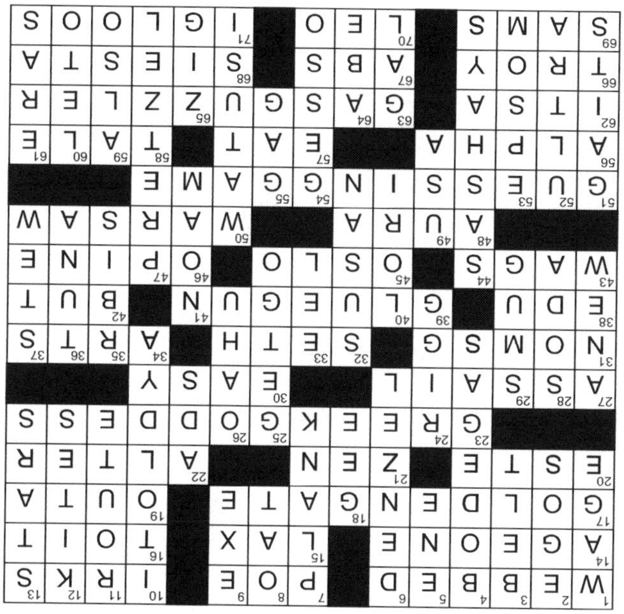

Puzzle 12

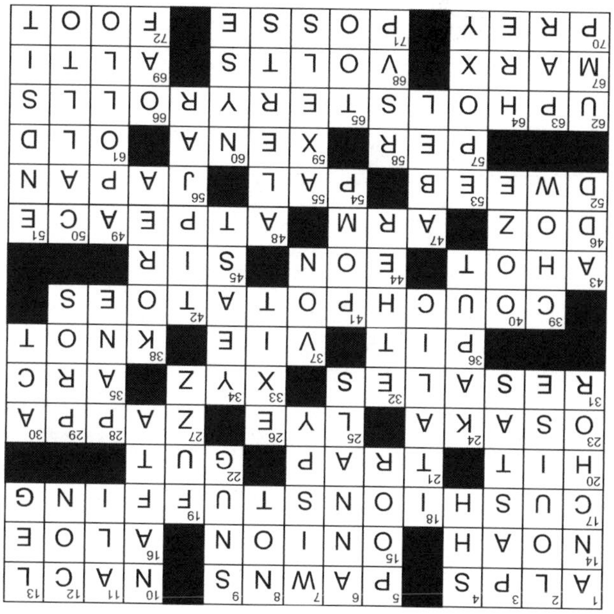

Puzzle 13

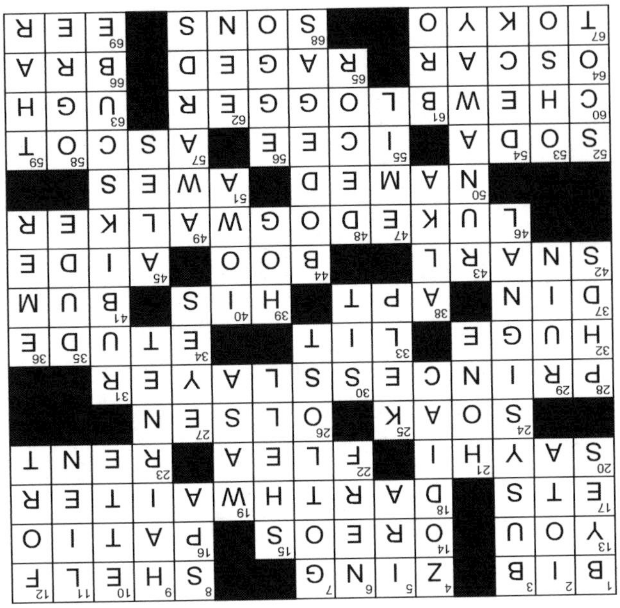

Puzzle 14

Puzzle 15

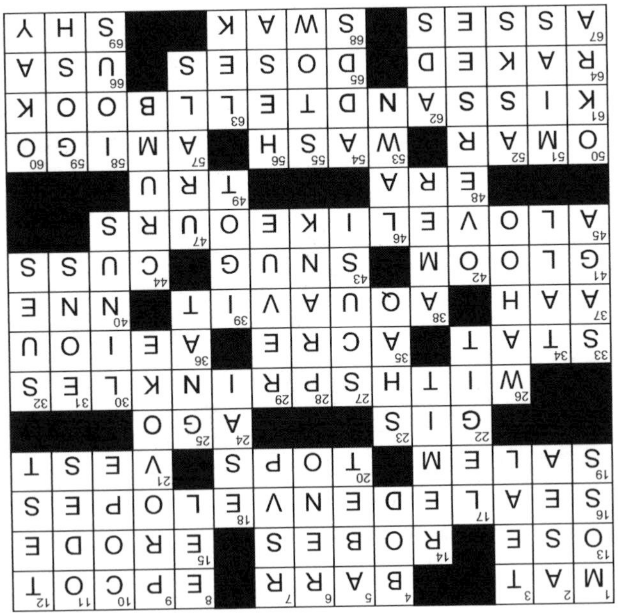

Puzzle 16

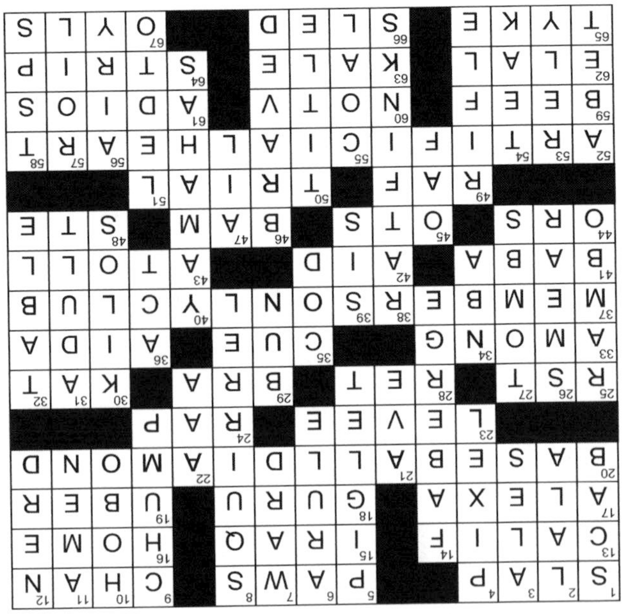

Puzzle 17

Puzzle 18

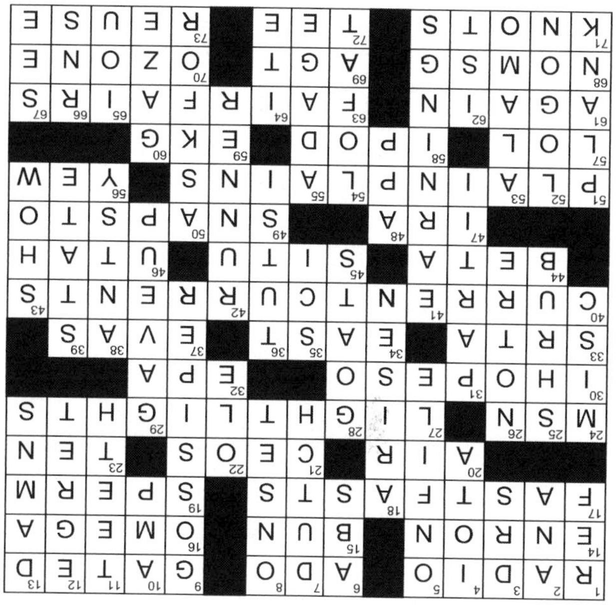

Puzzle 19

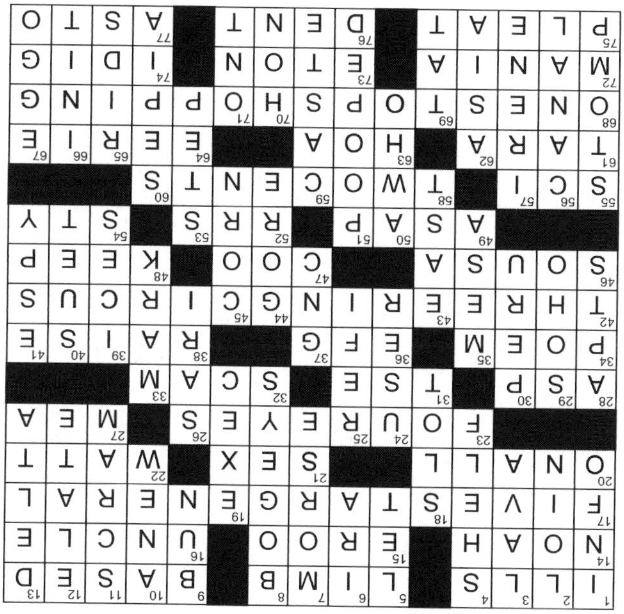

Puzzle 20

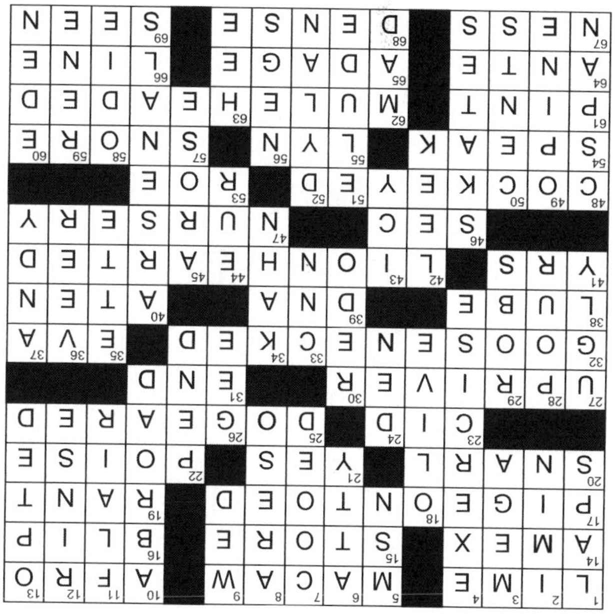

Puzzle 21

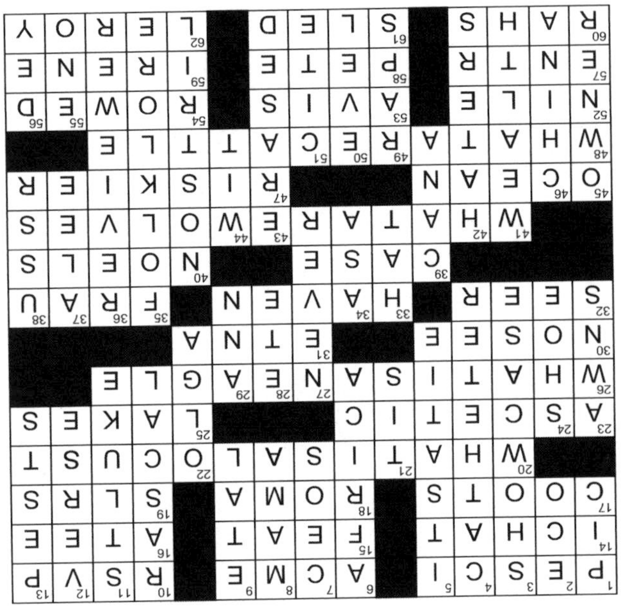

Puzzle 22

Puzzle 23

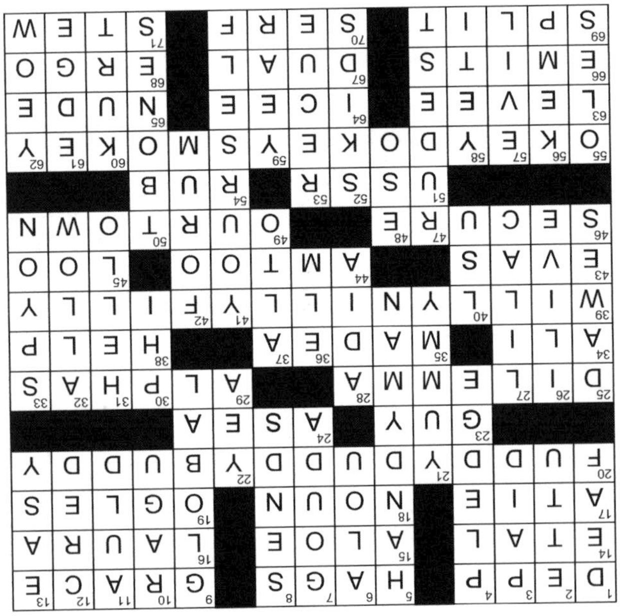

Puzzle 24

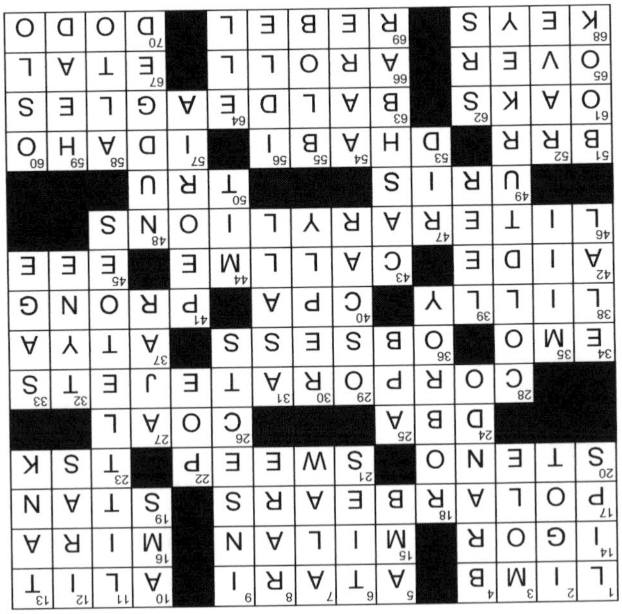

Puzzle 25

B	O	A	R	■	A	S	P	S	■	A	W	A	R	D
A	P	S	E	■	H	A	E	C	■	P	A	L	E	O
J	U	S	T	S	A	Y	N	O	■	E	R	A	S	E
A	S	T	R	O	■	S	A	L	E	■	H	M	O	S
■	■	■	I	N	C	O	L	D	B	L	O	O	D	■
A	S	I	A	G	O	■	■	■	A	O	L	■	■	■
L	O	L	L	■	B	O	L	E	Y	N	■	R	O	I
T	U	L	S	A	■	W	O	N	■	E	W	O	K	S
O	P	S	■	C	A	N	A	D	A	■	H	A	I	L
■	■	■	S	N	L	■	■	■	S	M	O	R	E	S
■	T	R	U	E	S	T	O	R	I	E	S	■	■	■
A	R	A	B	■	O	U	Z	O	■	S	T	A	B	S
L	A	I	T	Y	■	D	O	U	G	H	H	O	O	K
A	I	S	L	E	■	O	N	T	O	■	A	N	N	A
S	L	E	E	T	■	R	E	E	D	■	T	E	N	T

Puzzle 26

S	K	I	M	■	B	A	S	I	C	■	U	F	O	S
T	I	N	Y	■	A	T	A	L	L	■	P	O	R	E
R	E	S	T	■	R	O	S	S	I	■	H	U	G	E
I	F	I	H	A	D	A	H	A	M	M	E	R	■	■
N	E	D	■	S	S	S	■	■	B	U	R	L	A	P
G	R	E	E	K	■	T	O	W	■	G	E	E	S	E
■	■	■	S	T	A	■	T	O	E	■	■	A	H	A
■	■	U	P	O	N	T	H	E	R	O	O	F	■	■
H	A	N	■	■	A	B	E	■	R	C	A	■	■	■
A	L	B	U	M	■	A	R	P	■	E	R	U	P	T
S	A	U	N	A	S	■	■	O	L	A	■	S	U	E
■	■	T	H	E	C	A	R	P	E	N	T	E	R	S
N	A	T	O	■	A	S	I	A	N	■	A	F	I	T
I	D	O	L	■	R	E	P	R	O	■	L	U	N	E
B	O	N	Y	■	F	A	S	T	S	■	C	L	A	D

Puzzle 27

E	S	M	E	■	C	A	B	I	N	■	C	Y	A	N
L	A	O	S	■	H	A	I	K	U	■	R	A	R	E
B	U	L	L	M	A	R	K	E	T	■	E	K	E	S
O	D	E	■	A	L	O	E	■	R	E	P	E	A	T
W	I	S	E	M	E	N	■	F	I	L	E	T	■	■
■	■	■	F	A	T	■	B	L	E	S	S	Y	O	U
R	E	S	T	S	■	D	R	O	N	E	■	Y	I	N
A	L	A	S	■	B	E	A	S	T	■	H	A	L	T
N	B	C	■	P	A	W	N	S	■	T	O	K	Y	O
D	E	R	A	I	L	E	D	■	T	A	P	■	■	■
■	■	E	S	S	A	Y	■	T	O	S	S	U	P	S
M	E	D	I	A	N	■	S	U	I	T	■	S	U	P
O	R	C	A	■	C	A	T	T	L	E	C	A	L	L
L	I	O	N	■	E	L	A	T	E	■	U	G	L	I
D	E	W	S	■	D	E	B	I	T	■	B	E	S	T

Puzzle 28

T	B	A	■	S	I	P	■	M	G	M	■	F	A	B
S	E	N	A	T	O	R	■	A	R	E	■	E	R	A
K	A	N	G	A	R	O	O	R	A	T	■	N	O	G
S	N	A	R	L	■	■	S	I	N	■	A	C	M	E
■	■	■	E	L	E	P	H	A	N	T	S	E	A	L
C	O	M	E	S	T	O	■	■	Y	A	K	■	■	■
A	B	E	D	■	N	U	M	B	■	C	S	P	A	N
M	O	N	■	C	A	T	F	I	S	H	■	E	M	O
P	E	D	R	O	■	Y	A	D	A	■	F	R	O	S
■	■	■	I	N	A	■	■	E	N	G	L	I	S	H
S	P	I	D	E	R	M	O	N	K	E	Y	■	■	■
C	A	P	E	■	M	A	O	■	■	T	I	B	E	T
A	L	A	■	G	O	P	H	E	R	S	N	A	K	E
R	M	S	■	U	R	L	■	T	O	U	G	H	E	N
E	S	S	■	N	Y	E	■	S	T	P	■	A	D	D

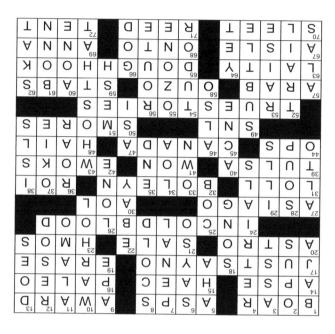

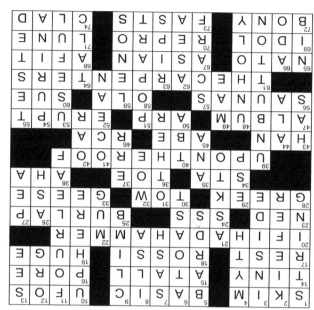

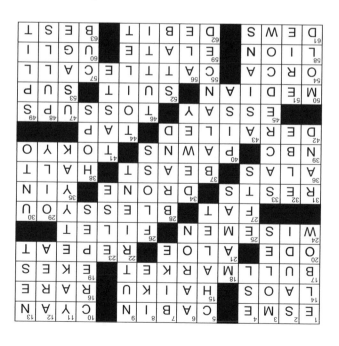

Puzzle 29

Puzzle 30

Puzzle 31

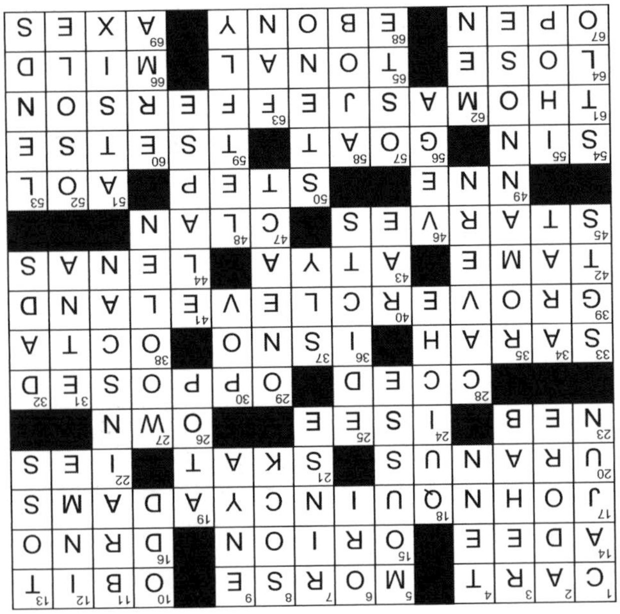

Puzzle 32

Puzzle 33

A	B	L	E	■	T	A	B	O	O	S	■	C	E	L
B	E	A	R	■	I	S	A	A	C	S	■	A	V	E
B	A	B	A	R	C	H	A	R	T	S	■	B	E	E
R	U	S	S	O	■	E	S	S	O	■	W	I	N	K
■	■	■	E	L	O	■	■	■	P	A	I	N	T	S
D	E	A	D	L	Y	B	A	S	I	N	S	■	■	■
O	W	L	■	■	S	E	C	T	■	T	H	U	G	S
L	E	A	P	S	■	A	H	A	■	S	Y	R	I	A
T	R	I	A	L	■	S	O	F	T	■	■	S	R	I
■	■	■	P	O	R	T	O	F	B	A	C	A	L	L
T	O	M	A	T	O	■	■	■	A	D	A	■	■	■
I	S	I	S	■	M	I	D	I	■	A	N	I	T	A
P	A	N	■	B	A	K	I	N	G	M	I	D	A	S
S	G	T	■	A	N	E	M	I	A	■	N	E	C	K
Y	E	S	■	T	O	A	S	T	S	■	E	A	T	S

Puzzle 34

B	E	L	A	■	L	A	M	B	■	U	M	B	E	R
I	C	A	L	■	O	H	I	O	■	M	I	A	M	I
C	H	I	L	L	P	I	L	L	■	B	L	A	C	K
S	O	D	O	I	■	■	N	E	A	R	■	E	E	E
■	■	■	F	E	N	D	E	R	B	E	N	D	E	R
A	L	I	■	S	A	O	■	O	S	L	O	■	■	■
B	A	C	K	■	M	O	W	■	■	L	T	G	O	V
C	R	E	A	T	U	R	E	F	E	A	T	U	R	E
S	A	T	Y	R	■	■	B	O	W	■	O	M	E	N
■	■	■	A	A	H	S	■	W	O	W	■	P	O	T
W	A	L	K	I	E	T	A	L	K	I	E	■	■	■
I	T	O	■	L	E	A	K	■	■	L	A	M	P	S
L	A	R	A	M	■	S	N	A	I	L	M	A	I	L
T	R	E	V	I	■	I	O	W	A	■	E	L	L	E
S	I	N	E	X	■	S	T	E	M	■	S	T	E	W

Puzzle 35

D	E	A	R	■	■	S	A	G	E	■	S	A	U	L
E	L	S	E	■	A	L	O	H	A	■	A	C	R	E
M	A	I	M	■	R	A	N	I	S	■	R	E	N	E
I	N	F	I	N	I	T	E	J	E	S	T	■	■	■
■	■	■	N	O	D	■	■	■	S	P	R	I	N	T
S	C	A	D	S	■	P	C	S	■	R	E	N	E	W
T	O	M	E	■	M	A	I	T	A	I	■	T	R	E
E	V	E	R	L	A	S	T	I	N	G	L	O	V	E
E	E	L	■	I	N	T	E	R	N	■	A	N	E	T
P	R	I	S	M	■	A	D	S	■	B	L	E	S	S
S	T	A	T	I	C	■	■	■	O	F	A	■	■	■
■	■	■	E	T	E	R	N	A	L	F	L	A	M	E
B	E	E	R	■	L	U	C	I	D	■	A	R	M	Y
O	G	L	E	■	T	S	A	R	S	■	N	E	V	E
Y	O	Y	O	■	S	E	A	S	■	■	D	A	I	S

Puzzle 36

B	E	R	G	■	A	M	P	■	■	W	H	A	M	O
O	V	A	L	■	S	A	I	D	■	H	U	M	A	N
M	E	G	A	P	H	O	N	E	■	O	N	I	C	E
B	R	U	N	O	■	■	U	M	P	S	■	S	H	U
■	■	■	C	H	A	M	P	I	O	N	S	H	I	P
G	A	Z	E	L	L	E	■	■	L	E	I	■	■	■
A	M	I	D	■	S	T	E	M	■	X	R	A	Y	S
Z	E	N	■	C	O	O	L	A	N	T	■	N	A	Y
A	N	G	E	L	■	O	K	R	A	■	A	T	M	S
■	■	■	T	U	G	■	■	S	T	Y	L	I	S	T
B	A	C	H	E	L	O	R	H	O	O	D	■	■	■
A	D	A	■	L	O	D	E	■	■	D	E	C	A	F
G	E	N	I	E	■	O	R	P	H	A	N	A	G	E
G	L	A	S	S	■	R	U	D	E	■	T	R	O	T
Y	E	L	L	S	■	■	N	A	M	■	E	D	G	E

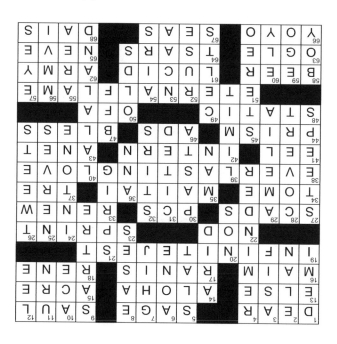

Puzzle 37

Puzzle 38

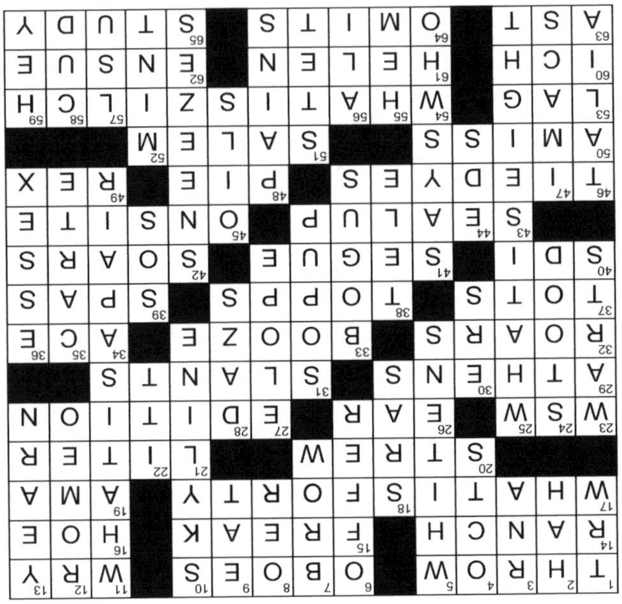

Puzzle 39

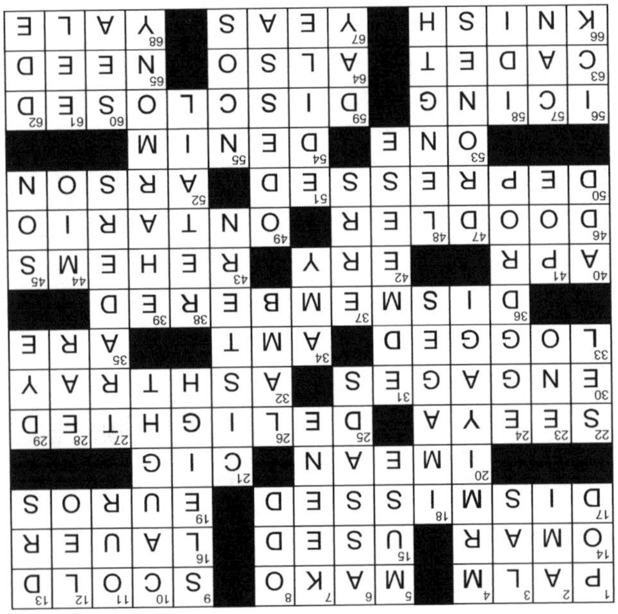

Puzzle 40

Puzzle 41

Puzzle 42

Puzzle 43

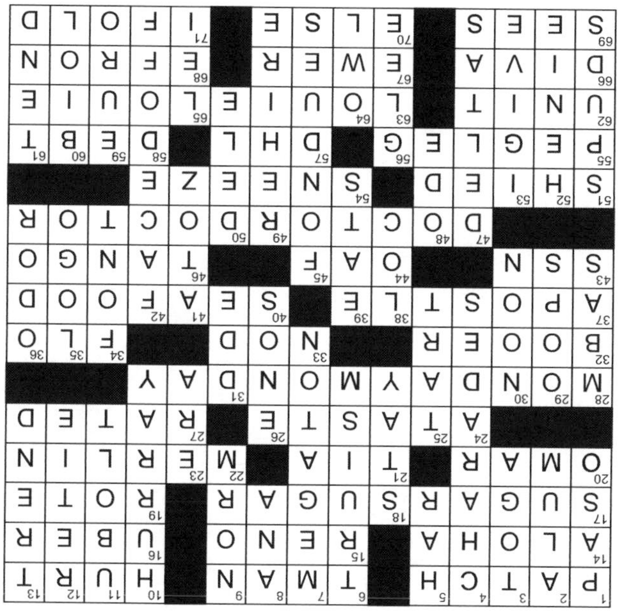

Puzzle 44

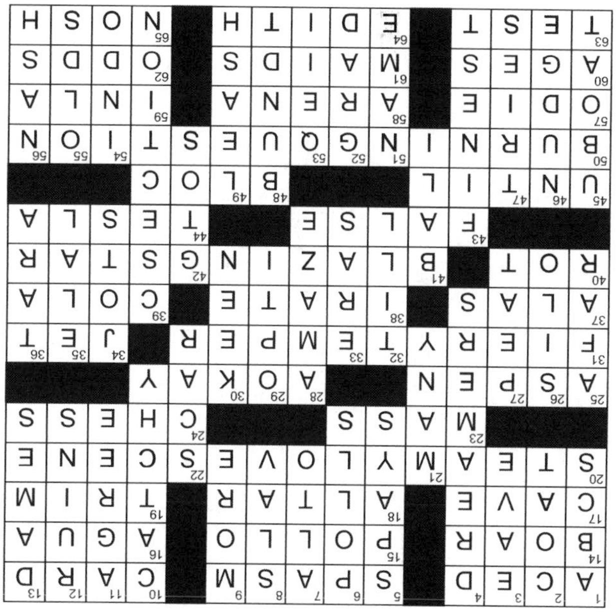

Puzzle 45

Puzzle 46

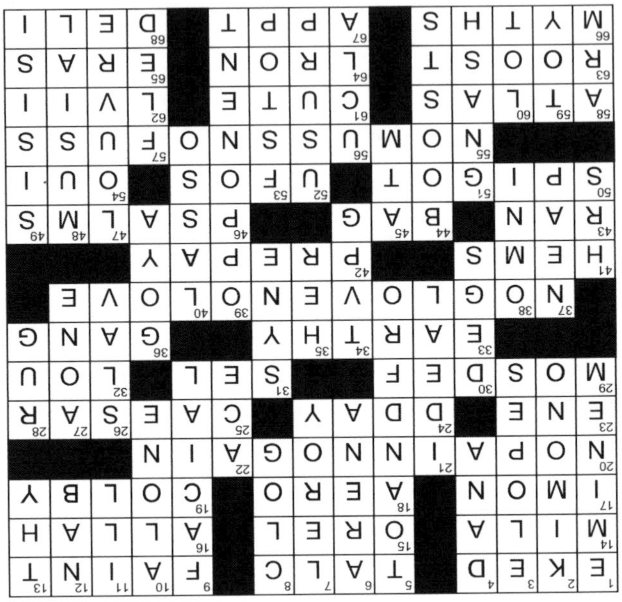

Puzzle 47

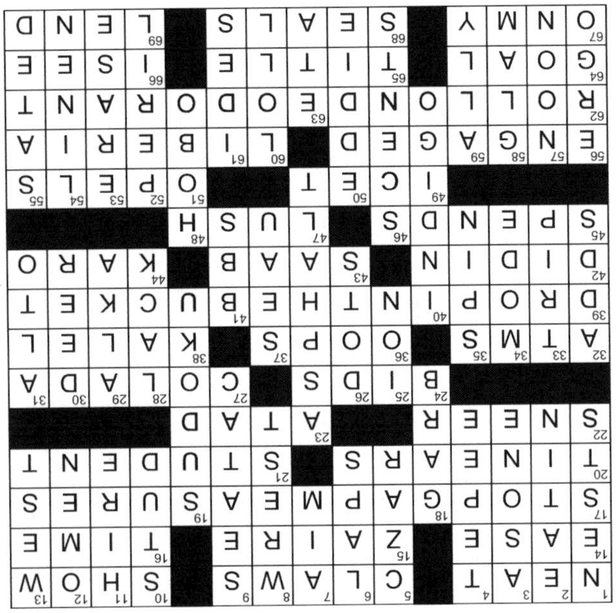

Puzzle 48

Puzzle 49

Puzzle 50

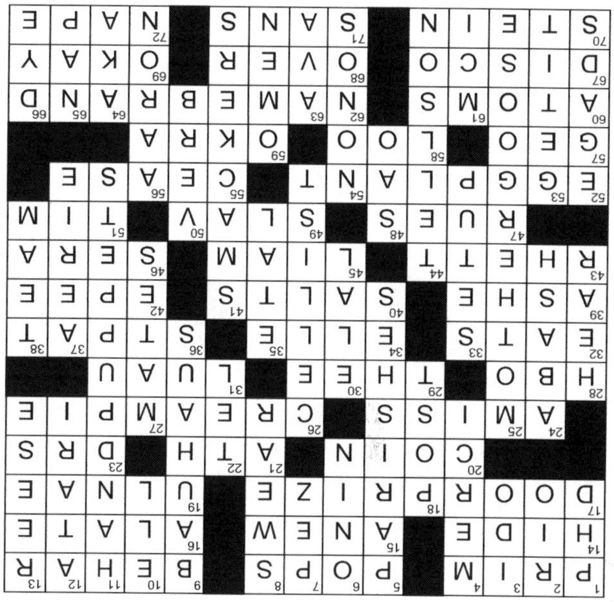

Puzzle 51

Puzzle 52

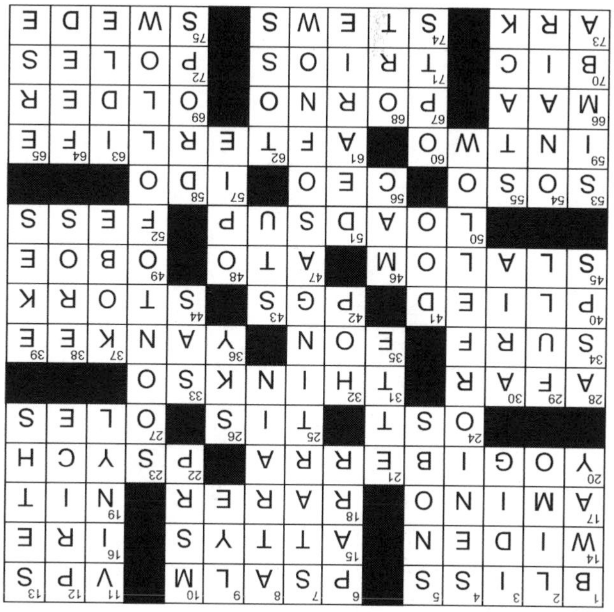

Puzzle 53

Puzzle 54

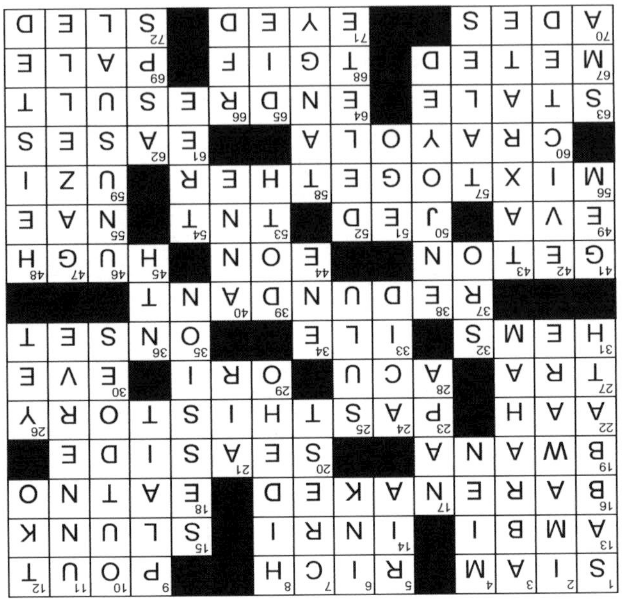

Puzzle 55

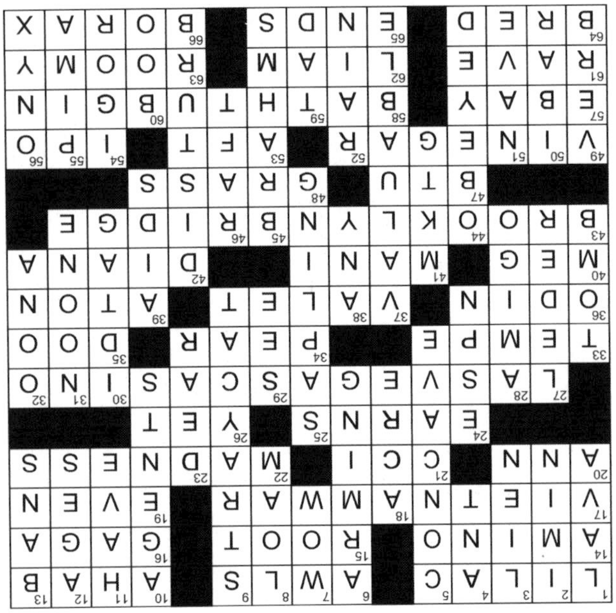

Puzzle 56

Puzzle 57

E	N	D	S	■	I	N	A	P	T	■	L	A	M	B
A	C	O	P	■	N	O	B	L	E	■	G	L	U	E
S	A	N	A	N	D	R	E	A	S	F	A	U	L	T
T	A	T	T	O	O	■	L	Y	T	E	■	M	C	S
■	■	■	■	M	O	B	■	■	F	L	A	S	H	Y
N	I	A	G	A	R	A	F	A	L	L	S	■	■	■
O	N	E	N	D	■	N	A	V	Y	■	S	H	I	P
D	O	R	A	S	■	A	T	A	■	S	I	E	V	E
S	N	O	W	■	A	N	A	T	■	C	S	P	A	N
■	■	■	A	P	P	A	L	A	C	H	I	A	N	S
I	N	S	T	E	P	■	■	R	O	O	■	■	■	■
C	E	O	■	D	O	S	E	■	R	O	C	K	E	T
H	A	W	A	I	I	A	N	I	S	L	A	N	D	S
A	T	E	N	■	N	U	R	S	E	■	S	E	E	P
T	O	D	D	■	T	R	Y	S	T	■	H	E	N	S

Puzzle 58

S	E	R	R	A	■	C	H	E	F	■	U	K	E	S
G	R	E	E	T	■	C	A	R	L	■	T	A	X	I
T	A	S	S	O	■	N	I	R	O	■	A	R	I	D
■	■	P	E	N	N	Y	M	A	R	S	H	A	L	L
G	R	E	E	C	E	■	■	N	I	T	■	T	E	E
N	I	C	K	E	L	A	N	D	D	I	M	E	■	■
A	M	T	■	■	L	Y	E	■	A	L	A	■	■	■
T	Y	S	O	N	■	E	A	R	■	L	E	P	E	W
■	■	■	B	A	D	■	T	E	N	■	■	E	V	A
■	■	G	I	V	E	N	O	Q	U	A	R	T	E	R
A	P	R	■	I	T	O	■	■	D	R	E	S	S	Y
C	H	A	N	G	E	O	F	H	E	A	R	T	■	■
T	A	P	E	■	S	N	I	T	■	M	E	O	W	S
U	S	E	S	■	T	A	F	T	■	I	N	R	E	D
P	E	S	T	■	S	N	I	P	■	S	T	E	T	S

Puzzle 59

E	C	O	L	■	■	S	L	A	W	■	S	C	A	T
L	O	M	A	N	■	S	O	R	E	■	P	O	L	O
B	R	A	Z	I	L	N	U	T	S	■	A	F	A	R
E	N	R	A	G	E	■	■	S	T	Y	■	F	I	N
■	■	■	R	E	A	T	A	■	S	I	R	E	■	■
■	■	T	U	R	K	E	Y	D	I	N	N	E	R	S
B	R	A	S	I	■	R	E	E	D	■	S	P	A	T
O	O	X	■	A	B	E	■	L	E	B	■	O	V	A
M	D	C	I	■	A	S	A	P	■	A	S	T	E	R
B	E	R	M	U	D	A	S	H	O	R	T	S	■	■
■	■	E	S	T	A	■	H	I	R	E	R	■	■	■
B	I	D	■	A	P	P	■	■	E	X	A	L	T	S
E	D	I	E	■	P	A	N	A	M	A	H	A	T	S
L	E	T	S	■	L	I	E	D	■	M	A	N	O	R
L	A	S	T	■	E	N	D	S	■	■	N	A	P	S

Puzzle 60

G	E	A	R	S	■	O	T	T	O	S	■	G	P	S
I	N	D	I	A	■	R	O	O	S	T	■	L	I	T
G	O	D	B	L	E	S	S	Y	O	U	■	E	A	R
A	S	S	■	A	F	E	E	■	■	D	O	N	N	A
■	■	■	I	A	L	R	E	A	D	Y	K	N	O	W
P	L	A	S	M	A	■	■	C	R	I	S	■	■	■
L	U	L	L	■	T	O	P	T	E	N	■	N	O	T
A	R	M	E	D	■	W	H	O	■	G	N	O	M	E
Y	E	S	■	E	Y	E	I	N	G	■	I	V	A	N
■	■	■	I	M	A	M	■	■	O	S	C	A	R	S
Y	O	U	R	E	W	E	L	C	O	M	E	■	■	■
A	T	S	E	A	■	■	O	R	E	O	■	E	R	R
R	T	E	■	N	O	T	H	E	Y	G	O	M	O	O
D	E	R	■	E	L	S	A	S	■	G	R	I	M	Y
S	R	S	■	D	E	A	N	S	■	Y	E	L	P	S

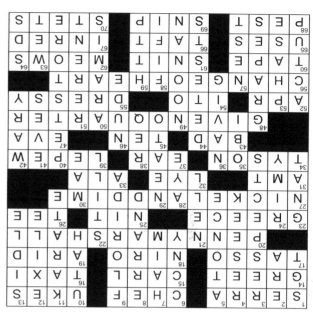

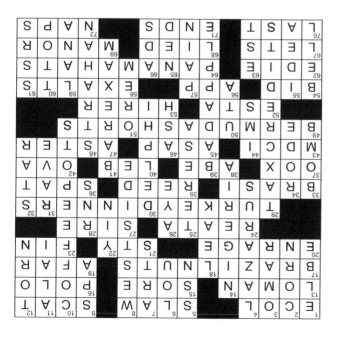

Puzzle 61

P	L	E	A	■	H	I	L	L	■	S	A	G	E	S
H	E	L	M	■	A	C	A	I	■	H	R	O	S	S
E	A	S	E	■	N	I	N	E	■	O	T	T	E	R
W	H	E	N	I	N	E	E	D	Y	O	U	■	■	■
■	■	■	■	G	A	S	■	■	A	I	R	I	E	R
■	■	R	I	G	H	T	T	U	R	N	O	N	L	Y
L	E	E	R	Y	■	■	W	I	N	S	■	M	A	D
A	L	F	A	■	A	M	I	S	S	■	R	A	T	E
M	I	I	■	U	N	I	T	■	■	D	E	T	E	R
A	S	L	O	N	G	A	S	I	L	I	V	E	■	■
S	A	L	O	M	E	■	■	P	O	O	■	■	■	■
■	■	■	M	O	R	E	T	H	A	N	O	N	C	E
H	I	P	P	O	■	G	O	O	F	■	B	O	O	S
O	S	C	A	R	■	A	N	N	E	■	E	G	O	S
O	A	T	H	S	■	D	E	E	R	■	Y	O	L	O

Puzzle 62

S	I	T	■	Y	O	D	E	L	S	■	L	A	T	E
U	N	O	■	A	V	E	D	O	N	■	O	D	I	N
B	T	W	■	C	A	L	I	C	O	Q	U	I	L	T
J	O	N	A	H	■	A	E	I	O	U	■	O	D	E
■	■	H	T	T	P	■	■	■	K	I	S	S	E	R
S	I	A	M	E	S	E	T	W	I	N	S	■	■	■
A	L	L	■	D	A	T	E	R	■	T	R	A	M	S
F	I	L	M	■	S	H	E	E	T	■	S	N	A	P
E	A	S	E	D	■	I	T	A	G	O	■	T	I	E
■	■	■	M	U	N	C	H	K	I	N	L	A	N	D
G	A	Z	E	B	O	■	■	■	F	E	A	R	■	■
U	S	O	■	A	S	B	A	D	■	O	P	C	I	T
P	E	R	S	I	A	N	G	U	L	F	■	T	O	E
T	E	R	I	■	L	E	A	P	O	F	■	I	T	S
A	D	O	S	■	E	G	R	E	T	S	■	C	A	T

Puzzle 63

A	D	S	■	B	E	A	R	D	■	U	M	B	E	R
K	A	T	■	A	L	C	O	A	■	T	I	A	R	A
I	R	A	■	L	A	M	A	R	■	U	N	C	A	P
M	R	B	U	T	T	E	R	W	O	R	T	H	■	■
B	I	L	L	I	E	■	■	I	N	N	■	E	P	A
O	N	E	P	M	■	L	A	N	D	■	A	L	A	N
■	■	■	■	O	S	L	O	■	E	S	C	O	R	T
■	■	B	A	R	T	C	R	O	C	K	E	R	■	■
B	O	O	M	E	R	■	T	I	K	I	■	■	■	■
R	O	X	Y	■	O	V	A	L	■	M	A	F	I	A
A	O	L	■	A	L	I	■	■	A	P	R	O	N	S
■	■	U	N	C	L	E	J	E	R	E	M	I	A	H
F	E	N	C	E	■	N	O	S	E	D	■	S	P	A
O	S	C	A	R	■	N	U	T	S	O	■	T	I	M
R	E	H	A	B	■	A	R	S	O	N	■	S	E	E

Puzzle 64

T	E	A	R	■	A	T	O	M	S	■	I	S	A	Y
A	N	N	A	■	W	O	V	E	N	■	M	A	T	E
L	E	T	S	■	E	R	A	T	O	■	A	C	E	S
C	R	O	C	O	D	I	L	E	R	O	C	K	■	■
S	O	N	A	R	■	■	■	R	E	M	■	C	S	I
■	■	■	L	E	G	O	S	■	■	I	S	L	E	S
A	W	W	■	M	U	S	K	R	A	T	L	O	V	E
B	O	Y	S	■	A	L	I	A	S	■	S	T	E	R
B	R	A	S	S	M	O	N	K	E	Y	■	H	R	E
O	S	T	E	O	■	■	S	E	T	U	P	■	■	■
T	E	T	■	L	I	E	■	■	■	R	A	I	T	T
■	■	E	Y	E	O	F	T	H	E	T	I	G	E	R
B	R	A	E	■	T	R	O	U	T	■	N	I	L	E
E	A	R	N	■	A	E	T	N	A	■	T	V	M	A
A	M	P	S	■	S	M	O	G	S	■	S	E	A	T

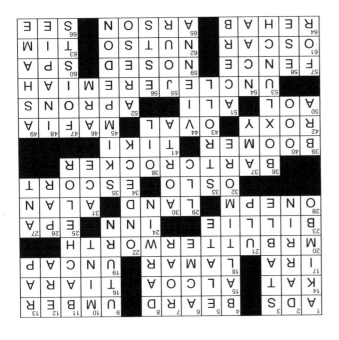

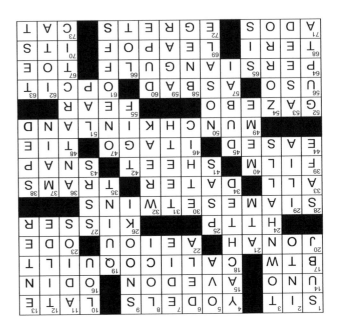

Puzzle 65

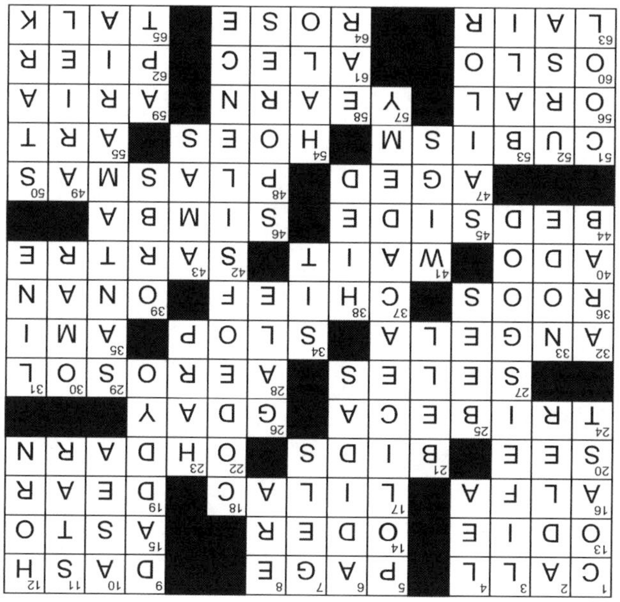

Puzzle 66

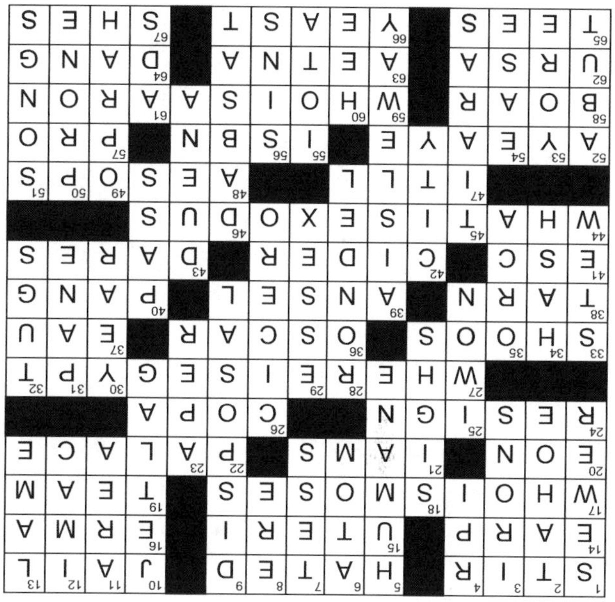

Puzzle 67

Puzzle 68

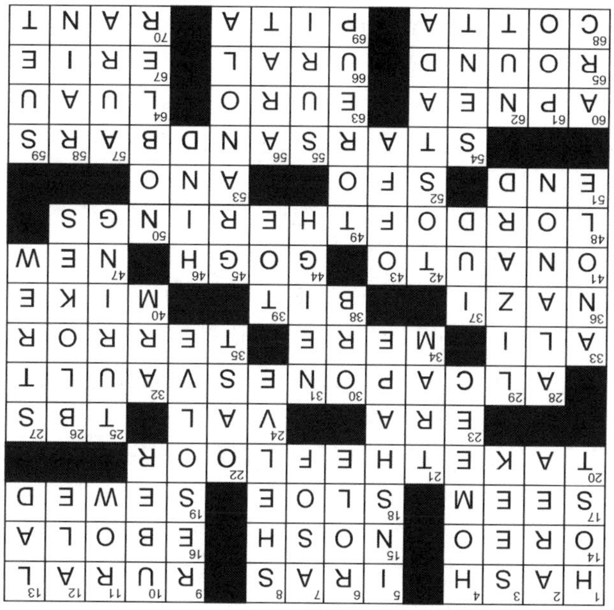

Puzzle 69

Puzzle 70

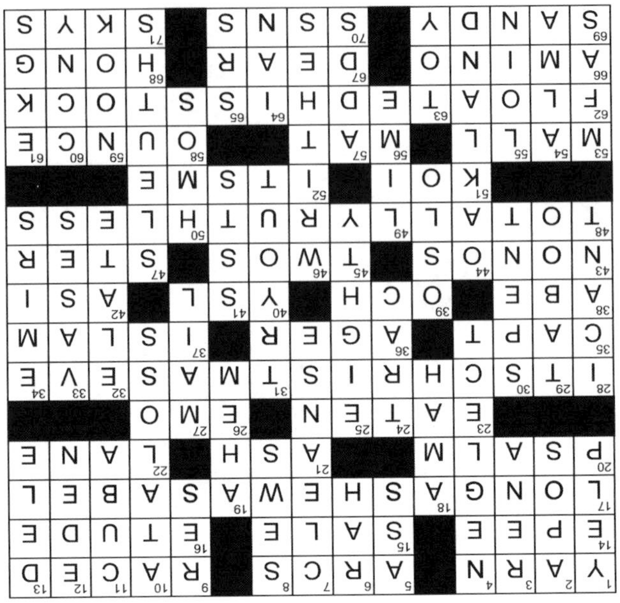

Puzzle 71

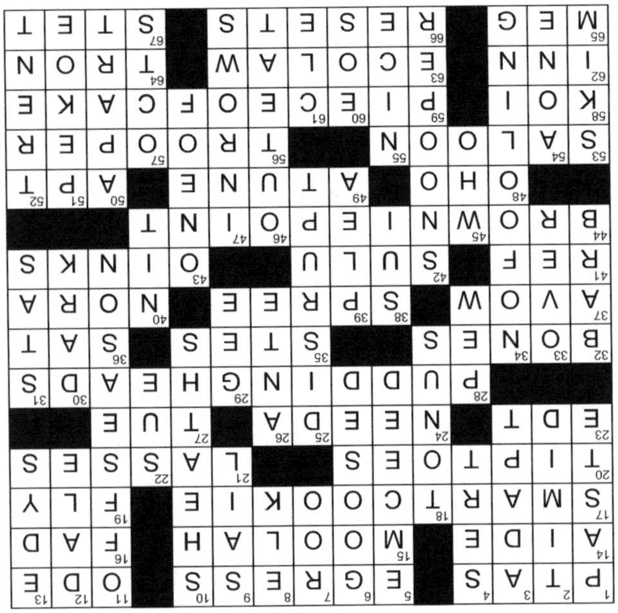

Puzzle 72

Puzzle 73

Puzzle 74

Puzzle 75

Puzzle 76

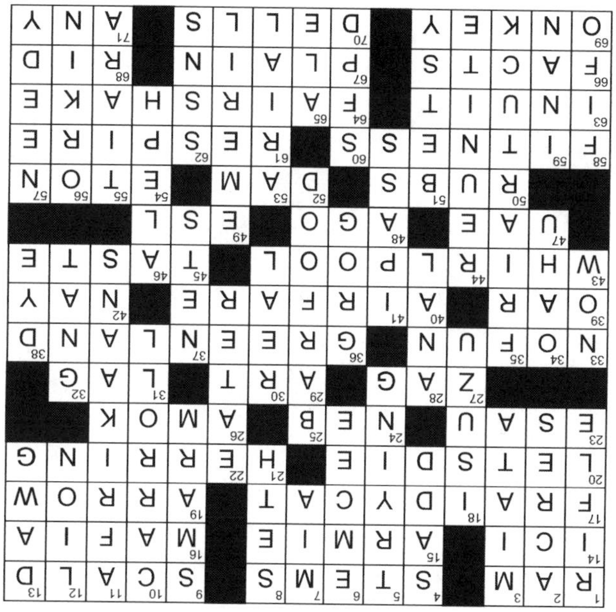

Puzzle 77

NUTSO CLAM SMUG
BRAWN LENO TIRE
ANDIE EVEN EAST
SAMSOFIWOJIMA
SEATS LONI
ABDUCT AID BSA
TROI TUTTI EOS
BATTLEOFTHEBAMS
ACT ANNOY ACME
TEE TDS RICHES
DUCT PLANK
ALLHAMSONDECK
OLIN BEAT IDEAS
LENA LILT GUSTO
EXES ERMA OPTED

Puzzle 78

SCABS ASAP SPEW
TORAH LIRA MIRE
OUTIE PREY OGRE
WRITETHESONGS
ESS PEA OLE TBA
RETRIM ATTIRE
OSPREY HEAR
AMTHEGREATEST
OREO SENDER
RUGRAT DAMMED
ETA NRA CUP AGE
BEGYOURPARDON
ONYX ORSO RADII
DATA UTEP TRESS
DEEM TARS YENTE

Puzzle 79

SLIP CARPE EYES
AIDE ULEES POLO
BLACKJACKPLAYER
RAH YOKOONO ONE
ECONO ENE VOCAL
PITA HERO
HONORSSTUDENT
DATE GULAG OTRA
IRA BONUSES EAR
ESTEE GRE HESSE
THOMAS SIXTHS
BUTTERPAT
CZAR RIVAL RITZ
OILY ARENA AREA
OTTO WENDY SEEP

Puzzle 80

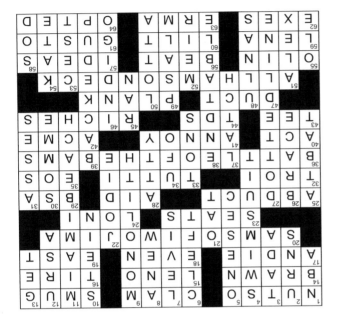

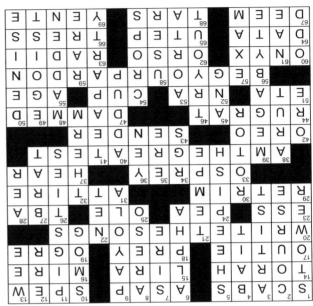

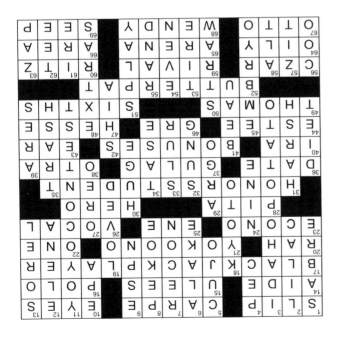

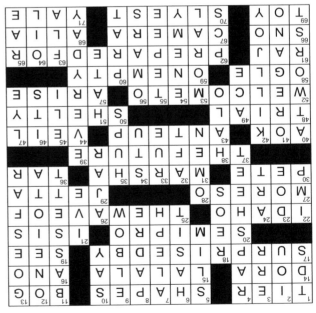

TIER SHAPES BOG
DORA LALALA ANO
SURPRISEDBY SEE
SEMIPRO ISIS
IDAHO THEWAVEOF
MORESO JETTA
PETE MARSHA TAR
THEFUTURE
AOK ANTEUP VEIL
TRIAL SHELTY
WELCOMETO ARISE
OGLE ONEMPTY
RAJ PREPAREDFOR
SNO CAMERA ALIA
TOY SLYEST YALE

Puzzle 81

Puzzle 82

Puzzle 83

Puzzle 84

Puzzle 85

Puzzle 86

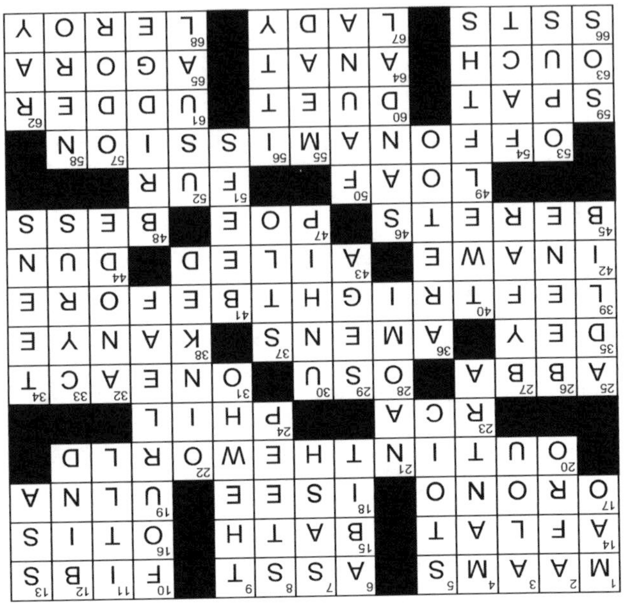

Puzzle 87

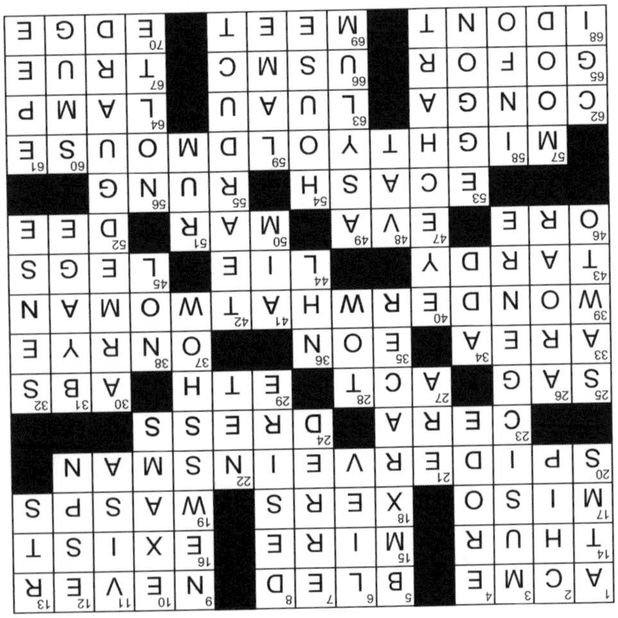

Puzzle 88

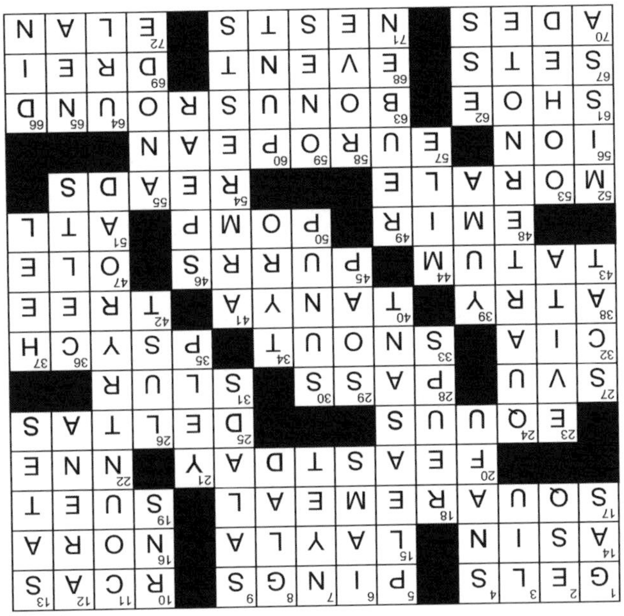

Puzzle 89

Puzzle 90

Puzzle 91

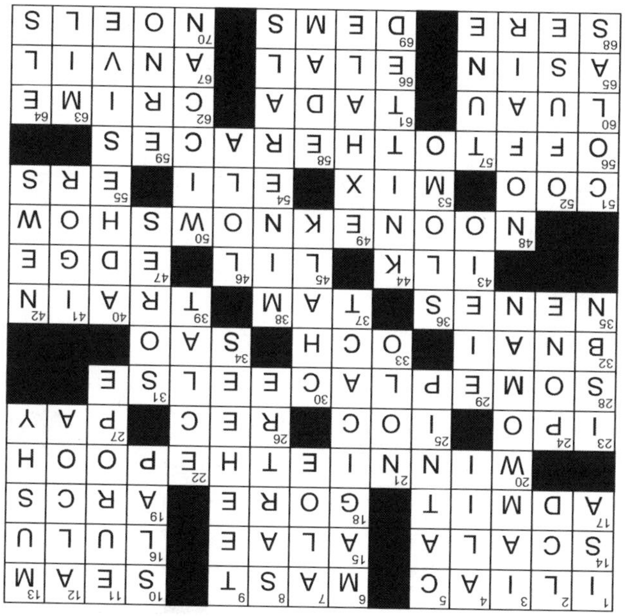

Puzzle 92

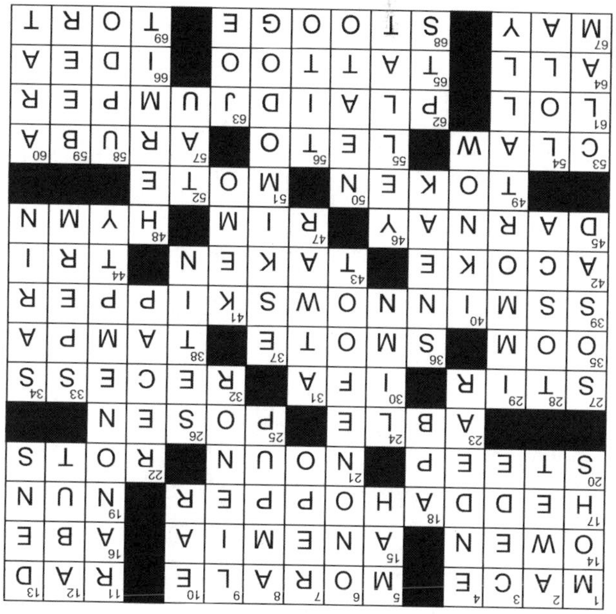

Puzzle 93

Puzzle 94

Puzzle 95

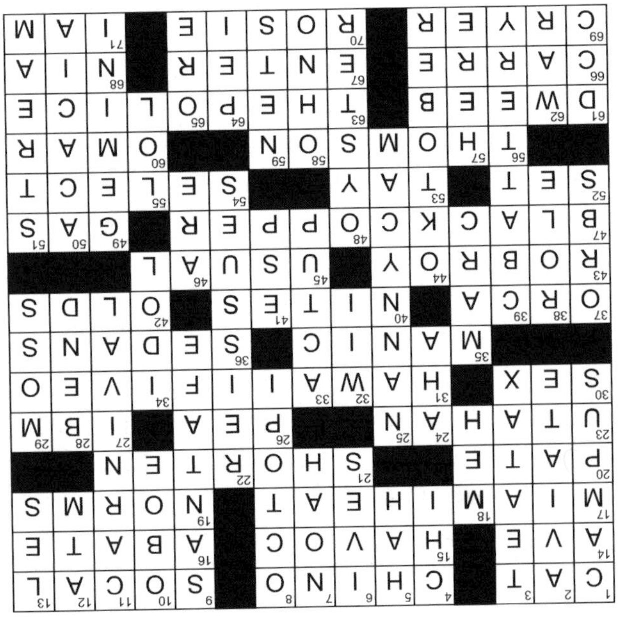

Puzzle 96

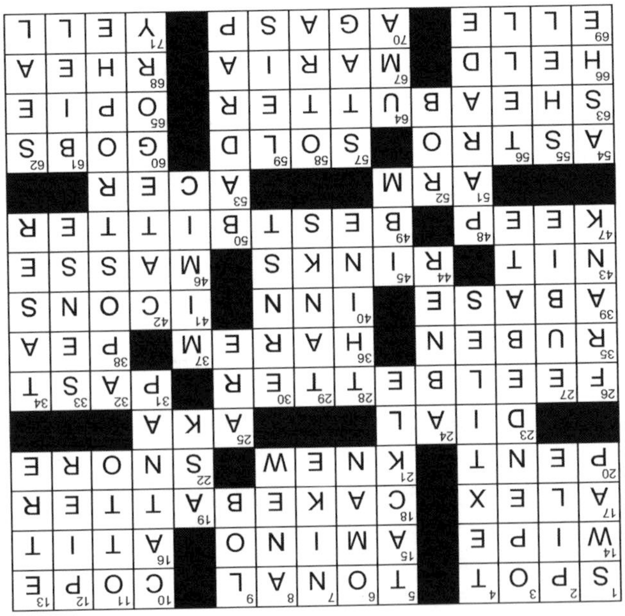

Puzzle 97

Puzzle 98

Puzzle 99

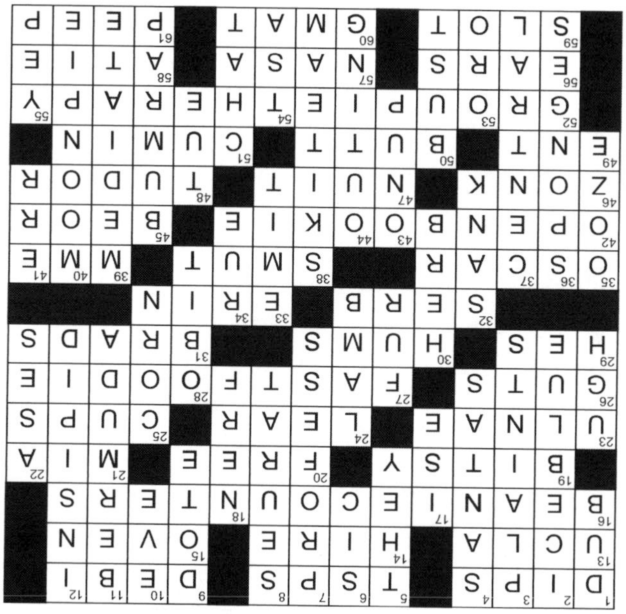

Puzzle 100

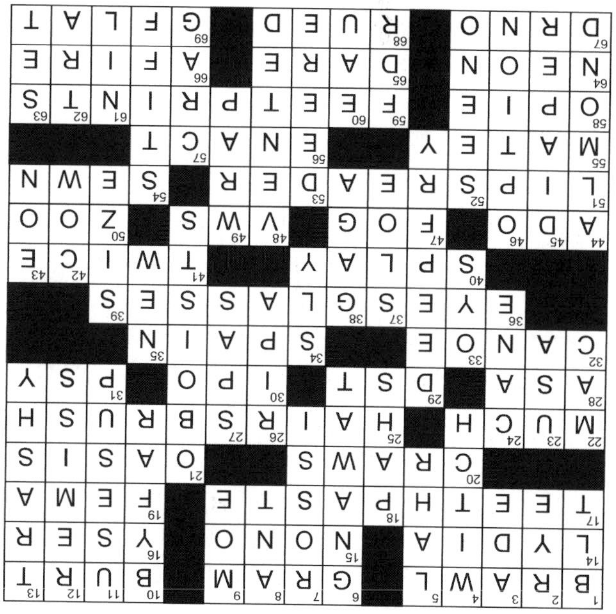

Puzzle 101

P	A	U	L	■	A	P	P	L	E	■	M	B	A	S
A	C	N	E	■	T	R	A	I	L	■	E	L	L	E
W	H	I	T	E	H	O	R	S	E	■	D	A	M	E
S	E	T	T	L	E	D	■	P	E	L	I	C	A	N
■	■	■	E	I	N	■	■	■	■	I	N	K	■	■
A	M	B	R	O	S	E	■	D	Y	N	A	M	I	C
V	A	L	E	T	■	R	A	R	E	E	■	A	S	A
E	G	A	D	■	T	A	L	O	N	■	S	G	T	S
R	O	C	■	M	O	T	T	O	■	S	T	I	L	T
Y	O	K	O	O	N	O	■	P	A	L	A	C	E	S
■	■	B	R	O	■	■	■	■	L	O	T	■	■	■
S	P	O	N	G	E	S	■	S	I	T	I	D	L	E
A	L	A	E	■	W	H	I	T	E	H	O	U	S	E
G	A	R	R	■	E	O	S	I	N	■	N	E	A	L
A	N	D	Y	■	R	O	A	R	S	■	S	S	T	S

46605968R00130

Made in the USA
Middletown, DE
30 May 2019